THE FINAL BOOK OF NERO AND SPORUS

Damnatio Memoriae

S.P. SOMTOW

Diplodocus Press · 2025

DAMNATIO MEMORIAE · 2

Damnatio Memoriae is the final volume of S. P. Somtow's series *Nero and Sporus*. Parts of this book originally appeared as a serial on Amazon Vella.

© 2025 by Somtow Sucharitkul
first published September 2024

paperback ISBN: 978-1940999-92-0
hardcover ISBN: 978-1940999-74-6

0 9 8 7 6 5 4 3 2 1

Damnatio
Memoriae

DAMNATIO MEMORIAE · 4

The Long Wait	9
Pluto and Proserpina	15
Lucius Junius Gallio	21
Clipped Wings	26
The Ring of the Death-God	33
The House of the Hetaira	39
Two Lives	46
Eleusis	52
Mysteries of Life and Death	59
Olympia	66
Chariots	75
Sacrifices	82
Songs without Words	90
Madness	96
Ubi Gaius Ego Gaia	103
Foreshadowings	111
The Sea	117
Triumph	121
Gaius Julius Vindex	131
Speaking to Gods	138
The Priestess of Claudius	145
A Place to Die	155
Imperatrix Reddux	167
Otho	175
The House of Petronius	181
Galba	191
Domus Aurea	199
Civil War	209
Bedriacum	219
Aulus Vitellius Germanicus	227
Persephone	233

DAMNATIO MEMORIAE · 6

πολλαὶ μορφαὶ τῶν δαιμονίων,
πολλὰ δ' ἀέλπτως κραίνουσι θεοί·
καὶ τὰ δοκηθέντ' οὐκ ἐτελέσθη,
τῶν δ' ἀδοκήτων πόρον ηὖρε θεός.
τοιόνδ' ἀπέβη τόδε πρᾶγμα

The gods may take a myriad shapes
and make the unexpected happen
that which we think does not come to pass
instead the gods bring the unthought into being
as all can see

— Euripides

DAMNATIO MEMORIAE · 8

Primus in orbe
deos fecit
timor

In this world
it was fear that first
created the gods

— Petronius

I

THE LONG WAIT

I'm remembering the sea again. I thought I smelled it yesterday. But no: they were just flooding the arena for a sea battle, and the searing sun has sucked up all the water now.

Now I only smell sand, blood, and the shit of wild beasts. I've been alone overnight; but now they've moved me to a "superior" accommodation as befits my divine status. It is on an upper level; there's even a view of the Circus, little more than a slit of dusty, hot light. It lets in and stench, too.

It was not exactly cool during the night, just not as searing as the day. The air was oppressive, damp. They brought in a couch for me, but kept one foot chained to the wall, though escape was hardly an option. Breakfast was stony bread, salt, garum, and a handful of olives.

Then that makeup artist returned.

But it's more than a touchup. My execution has been delayed again and my face is no longer pristine.

They tell me that this time the games have been extended for one hundred days. Why not? There have already been three coronations this year, and a few near-coronations. A lot to celebrate. And a lot of misery — taxation, the bread dole being cut, the hottest summer in memory — a lot of anguish to assuage, a riled-up mob ready to riot.

Imagine the collective sigh, the release of pent-up passions from tens of thousands of voices, as they watch a goddess being ravished to death in the arena by a brutish monster.

But why did *I* have to be their goddess?

***

Good news, Divinitas.

I'm finally getting my death scene? I've waited long enough, with only you for company.

You got me into makeup *days* ago, but instead of a quick death in front of over a hundred thousand screaming admirers, you've lured me into telling my life story. From peasant boy captured by pirates to plaything of a famous satirist. From slave to slaveowner with estates confiscated from great aristocrats. From freedman to imperial concubine. From man to woman. I've told you all these things, not to get them off my chest, but because one must do something to fill the time.

Everyone thinks the arena is all fast-paced excitement, but for us, the entertainment, it is an endless, stupefying orgy of *waiting*. Putting on makeup. Getting dressed up. Sitting through the reshuffling of schedules when the star gladiator has a cold, or a giraffe goes missing, or the lions are too sated to eat any Chrestianoi. Believe me, I would welcome another diversion, even if it's my own execution.

Don't tell me it's *another* delay.

Well, Goddess ... a brief delay. News is, Vespasian is marching on Rome. News is, Vespasian views you a little more favorably than Vitellius. News is, if we could get word to him....

I would be surprised if he remembered me. I hardly knew him. He showed up at the party, you know, the one in which Statilia Messalina's husband was made to commit suicide. He also came to one of Himself's performances in Greece ... and committed the worst possible insult ... he nodded off.

The Emperor — I mean the Divine Nero, not the one who has condemned me to death — was not happy. Vespasian would have been permanently exiled somewhere, if he hadn't proved useful in putting down the Judaean revolt.

Well, it looks as if there is a glimmer of hope for you. Vespasian has been declared Emperor by our legions in Egypt and Judaea. It appears that he is marching on Rome.

Doesn't mean much. Everyone and his uncle has marched on Rome this year, and so far only Galba, Otho, and Vitellius got to be Emperor. Why make this the year of *four* emperors? Three is much more of a sacred number. Three Fates. Three Graces. Three Muses —

Nine, actually.

Nine. Right. How long does it take to get here from Judaea? By land or by sea? A month? *Six* months? Is he fighting the forces of Vitellius on his way? I don't suppose he'll just march right over and kick Vitellius off his throne? Even in the unlikely event that he knows or cares who I am, Vespasian is not going to arrive in time to save me. Though the sight of a grizzled general riding heroically into the Circus Maximus at the head of his legions to rescue the most beautiful boy-girl-Empress-goddess would, I am sure, be quite the climax.

And the crowd loves plot-twists.

Do you dare to hope, Sporus?

No.

Then at least tell me more. Tell me about Greece.

Oh yes. Olympus and Hades rolled into one.

You left me hanging. Nero had finally ordered you unmanned, to bring you closer to the image of Poppaea. You passed out from the pain, and you woke up on a ship, bound for Greece.

You tell the story then! If you know so much.

But I want to know so much more....

Damnatio Memoriae · 14

II

Pluto and Proserpina

The sea …
    I woke in the arms of a god.
    My wounds had not healed, but a god does not have to wait for the passing of a mortal's pain. I woke to Himself whispering in my ear, "Poppaea, Poppaea, Poppaea."

"Lucius," I said, moaning softly. It drove his passion; each thrust sharpened my pain. I longed to go to another place, any place, because of the pain, and because my body had not yet healed, but the god was impatient.

Perhaps I passed out, because I was propelled into some kind of dream. It was the same dreamworld where I sometimes encountered Hyacinth after his death.

In dreams we do go to other worlds. Dreams are not mere flights of imagination.

I stood in a dry, dark place. It was utterly cold until I felt the shade of Hyacinth, a warm breath gusting in my face for just a moment.

Come.

He took my hand. We floated over stony ground. Now and then the dead looked up at us, but mostly they kept to the shadows. There was no sun. Even the sky seemed made of stone.

Come, Hyacinth repeated, in the language of my childhood, calling me by a name I had almost forgotten, my true name.

I called him by his, too.

This place, I thought, it's not the place where we were taught, as children, we would go. I remember tales of feasting and warriors, not stone-gray emptiness. Not this desolation, this heartbreak. This was a Roman kind of afterlife, shadowy and full of regret. *Facilis descensus Averno,* I thought. Going down to Hell is the easy part. Climbing back up, on the other hand....

"Where are you taking me?" I whispered.

"To meet my dominus," said Hyacinth.

The stone floor inclined. We were descending down a kind of cave or tunnel. A cold wind wuthered. The tunnel seemed endless, yet I was descending swiftly, as though I were being sucked in by a ravenous predator. Though there was barely any light there was a searing cold, creeping up from the stone floor, from the damp walls. It was not the cold that is the absence of heat, but the cold of old corpses, of soullessness.

Follow, Hyacinth said again, and now even his breath contained no warmth.

Presently the tunnel widened, and I found myself in the throne room of the Lord of the Dead.

There was a court full of flitting shadows, their robes woven from darkness. They whispered and buzzed, like insects in a summer night. Sconces with torches from which emanated a cold blue fire lined the walls. In the distance, on thrones made from human skulls, sat the King and Queen of the Underworld.

Time moved differently in the dreamscape. Suddenly I was standing at the foot of the twin thrones. Hades stared down at me, and I saw who he really was.

"Divinitas," I whispered.

"It's true," said Death. "There is no escape."

He smiled. His voice, perfectly modulated, echoed and floated on the chill air as though he were reciting Euripides. And then I saw who had become Queen of the Dead.

"Yes," she whispered, she who gazed at me with haunting eyes, *my* eyes, who smiled *my* smile; "I am so sorry," she said softly. "In the end, you are just an innocent boy. Many have died already because of you. Many more will die. But you have had no say in any of it."

I knelt at the feet of Proserpina, the death-goddess, who was also the Lady Poppaea Sabina, whose perfect face was the source of all my suffering.

"I am not here forever, you know," she went on. "Another will take my place one day, and reign from this throne of bones. I think," and she called me by name in my own language, the one only Hyacinth had known, "I think it will be you."

Her gaze seemed to steal my soul. I began to weep.

And then it was that I felt pain again, a swooping pain that made the tears spurt still more, and I cried out in terror and desolation; I felt myself coming awake and I knew that it was the god violating me, my flesh as well as my soul.

And Nero Claudius Caesar Augustus Germanicus cried out as well, believing, I am sure, that he was giving me pleasure, for surely it must be a blessing to be raped by a god.

***

So the days passed, the Divinity hardly leaving me alone except to eat, drink, or work on the grand composition he intended to inflict upon Greece. Unhealed, my battered body taking on more hurt. And always, I feigned enjoyment. Dreaming or awake, it was all Hell to me.

But the gods are easily bored, and it was twelve days by the time we arrived in Corinth. I was afraid he would take Hylas for his amusement, but it appeared that I, the improved, more compliant reincarnation of Poppaea, had actually driven him to exhaustion.

On the eleventh day he told me he needed time to commune with his muse. I spent the day working with Hylas to try to improve his Greek; his Latin had become pretty passable. The Divinitas did not summon me even in the middle of the night.

***

It was night again when we reached Corinth, arriving, it seemed, almost in secret. We were met by some official and swiftly escorted to a villa whose owners, it seemed, had been temporarily dispossessed, not far from the Temple of Octavia; for this Corinth was not the Corinth of ancient legend, but the Corinth re-founded by Julius Caesar a century after it had been razed to the ground and its entire population sold into slavery ... to teach the Achaean League a lesson. Our litters moved quickly; I did not sit with the Emperor but followed, with Hylas walking beside the drawn curtain.

The quarters were sumptuous enough, though this was not Rome. The house was in Roman style, with a small atrium. There were plenty of slaves in attendance, but they did not seem very happy. They stood about, eyes downcast, uncertain. The official, who had not even introduced himself, left hurriedly, saying that there would be a proper delegation in the morning.

Indeed, it was left to the boy Epictetus to get things set up, since the lad was the most high-ranking member of the Emperor's household in the absence of Imperial Secretary Epaphroditus —who had to manage the Empire on behalf of Statilia, poor thing! — and he limped about the hallway, ordering the slaves to do busy work. Presently he turned to the more experienced Croesus to help him, so that my household was actually managing the domestic arrangements for the Divine Emperor Himself.

Nero was led away to what was presumably the grandest cubiculum in the house, and when I made to follow, he waved me away. "We're in Greece now," he said. "Women know their place here." To Epictetus said, "Go find your Divine Mistress a proper veil, in case any strangers drop in."

So I found myself standing awkwardly in the foyer, staring up at the death masks of noble Romans I did not recognize, presumably the ancestors of whoever had vacated the premises for the duration.

"Well," I said to Croesus, "perhaps it won't be quite so bad here in the homeland of Aeschylus and Plato. Respectable wives don't go to dinner, and I am sure Himself will need to go to many symposia."

Croesus said, "I can't imagine you sitting at a loom all day while Himself is out performing for his raving admirers. If he doesn't need Poppaea, he'll definitely need Sporus. And Sporus will sit well with the Greeks."

"But Sporus is forever broken," I said.

"Who you are," Croesus said, "is in your soul, and in your heart, young domine."

I did not answer. I did not believe him.

An old slave was polishing a bust. A balding man, perhaps in his fifties. "You," I said. "Is this the owner?"

The slave cowered.

I said, "You can speak freely."

"Domine," he said, "are we all going to be crucified?"

"Whyever would you say that?"

Croesus whispered in my ear: "You know that under Roman law, if a slave kills his master, every slave he possessed is always crucified. It's the deterrent that holds together the entire fabric of Roman society. Deep down, it's the fear of their own slaves that motivates them."

"Then why did I feel so powerless?"

"Do you still?"

I nodded.

"Yet you are free."

I said to the old slave, "If you're going to be crucified, I can't really help you; you may as well tell me what's going on here — why everyone looks so glum, why we were brought here in such haste — why the governor did not meet us in the harbor."

III

Lucius Junius Gallio

"We did not kill our master," said the old slave, who was named Hector, "but it is whispered that they simply will say that we did not prevent his death — and therefore murdered him by omission."

Croesus took me aside. "This house belonged to Lucius Junius Gallio Annaeanus," he said. "The proconsul of the province. He should have greeted us at the harbor, but he has committed suicide."

I racked my brain, trying to place the name. At last, I vaguely recalled him. "Seneca's brother," I said. "So, a traitor, then." He might even have ridiculed Nero's poetry in an indiscreet moment.

"He must have thought the Emperor was coming to see to his execution in person."

The old slave said, "It's the inheritance, Empress." Clearly. If he killed himself, Gallio would be considered to have died honorably, and his estates would pass by law to his heirs. But if he were put to death for treason he would forfeit everything. "Murder would be a gray area, wouldn't it?" I said. "He had not *yet* been found guilty of insurrection. The Emperor could still seize his lands ... and to make sure the letter of the law was adhered to, all the slaves would have to be crucified ..."

"A precautionary measure. An Empire is only as good as its paperwork."

Despite its madness, Rome runs with a relentless logic. You can see it from its language: number, mood, tense, aspect, person, case ... lining up like soldiers to produce the precise ending each word requires. They love Greek, because Greek has rules too, but it has vagueness, ambiguity, and an inherent ability for any sentence to simultaneously mean its opposite.

"Precautionary?" I said. "But isn't it inhumane?"

Croesus smiled a thin, sad smile. He did not have to explain. The word "inhumane" is not used of slaves, because they aren't quite human; Aristotle calls them "animate property." It was a truth I knew intimately.

But I knew, too, that even the free are not free.

"You're going to speak to Nero about it, aren't you?" said Croesus. "Don't. It won't make a bit of difference."

"Where are the proconsul's heirs, his children?" I asked.

Hector said, "They are in hiding, Divinitas. Up north, I think. They did not tell us exactly where."

It seemed I had not left Rome at all. Not the stifling whispers, not the ever-present fear of the Emperor's wrath, not the constant conspiracies. I stood there in the entrance hall of the villa, not having been told where I was to stay or where my slaves should put my things. Other slaves emerged, looking at me, curious, perhaps wanting to plead with me, though I was powerless. It was awkward.

***

After a time, Himself emerged, all purple and gold, perfumed and freshly made up. He was accompanied by guards. "We're off to visit Corinth's most famous *hetaira*," he said. "Thaïs."

"I should get properly dressed," I said.

"Oh, you're staying home," said the Divinity. "A *hetaira*'s lair is too permissive a place for the wife of an Emperor. There'll be lewd talk, drunkenness, and lots of poetry reading; nothing that should interest a lady."

"Why can't I go as a boy?"

"Because we are God-Emperor and Empress, dearest Poppaea," he said. "And your pretty head doesn't need to be polluted with philosophy."

"Aren't *hetairai* ladies?" I said.

"As much as delicati are boys," said the Emperor. Again, his tone seemed devoid of irony.

"Before you go, Lucius ..." I began.

"Have a nice rest," he said. "After all, in your condition ..."

I didn't know if he was toying with me or whether he was in fact in a state of delusion.

"Since I am, as you say, in some kind of 'condition', my beautiful Lucius ..."

"Oh! My sweet wifey wants a gifty-wifty?" Was this cloying sweetness more delusion? Or was it all calculated? Or, worse, the prelude to some violent outburst? After my vision of Pluto and Proserpina in the underworld, I no longer cared whether I lived or died.

"Can't you seize the estate *without* killing all the slaves?" I blurted out.

"It's not like you to meddle in politics, Poppaea," Nero

said, and I *knew* that was untrue.

I could not appeal to reason, but perhaps venality would work. I said, "A man like Gallio must have slaves of the best quality. It would be a waste to kill them."

"You're right," said the Emperor. "But when a slave turns against his master, you have to kill them all. If you don't, we'll have another Spartacus ... all society would collapse."

"You mean to say, with all the fierce German tribes, the implacable Parthians, the constantly revolting Jews, Rome is more afraid of a few housemaids? Divinitas, *I* was a slave. Did you ever fear me?"

The Emperor seized me by the shoulders. He looked deep into my eyes. I thought I saw a single tear on his cheek. "O Goddess," he said, "you are to be feared more than armies, more than a tempest."

He kissed me with such passion that I thought he would forget about the soirée at the *hetaira*'s.

Then, abruptly, he broke away, leaving me with the taste of wine and rose-water on my tongue. "I suppose I can bend the rules a little," he said. Crooking his little finger, he summoned Croesus. "Make sure the paperwork is impeccable," he said, "I don't want Gallio's children to accuse me of reckless confiscation. I'm a reasonable God."

"Thank you, Lucius," I said, "for humoring your little wifey."

"We'll have to crucify a few, mind you," he said. "Make a big show of it and somehow let the rest slip through the cracks."

"Which ones?" Croesus said.

"I suppose the least valuable. Just kill the old ones. We wouldn't be able to sell them, anyway."

At this, Hector the old, and probably the most loyal, let out a terrified groan. I had not managed to save him.

"I'll make sure the deed is properly drawn up for the villa," Croesus said.

"Oh, I don't need another villa," said the Emperor. "Poppaea, dear, you take it."

"I don't need a villa either," I said, wondering if the shade of the old slave would haunt me if I ever took possession.

"Nonsense, my dear. Just think of it as a wedding gift."

IV

Clipped Wings

And just like that, my Lord and Master went out into the night, escorted by a dozen guards, purpled and perfumed so that none could mistake his identity.

And I was left behind in another luxurious mansion I did not care to own. Here I was, in the epicenter of the known world's culture, but I was barred from participating in its riches, because I was now a woman.

I eventually found my room, which was capacious enough. A fresco of the three Graces adorned one wall. Otherwise the furnishings were simple, though costly.

Croesus would have to do all the documents for the seizure of Gallio's estates (and gifting me the villa) … so he was busy cataloguing the property, including the slaves, which apparently were also mine now. Perhaps there would be some good musicians, or a decent scribe; though I had become fluent in many languages, and I read well, I had never been able to form any letters other than crudely.

Time passed. I paced. I knew that the Divinitas would

not be back until morning — or even later.

I was sad about Hector, even more so when he insisted on coming to my chamber to thank me for attempting to save him. He was in tears. "The domina never learned our names," he said. "All she ever wanted was to go back to Rome. She didn't enjoy being sequestered at all; the local highborn women are used to it. About once a month, out of sheer boredom, she would have us all beaten. But you, mistress …"

"I'm not your mistress," I said sharply.

"So it's true, then. The rumor. That you are not actually the Lady Poppaea Sabina."

"Does it matter?" I said bitterly. "The gods make their own reality."

"Well, I shan't be spreading such rumors; I'll be strung up and being pecked at by carrion birds."

I motioned for Hylas, who knew how to be invisible until he was wanted, to pour me a *krater* of wine, and a second for Hector. He was no longer weeping; he seemed to have reconciled himself to dying in agony for no real reason but to fulfil some bureaucratic requirements. What could I do for him?

"I'll tell them to give you a draught beforehand. And not to use nails."

"Thank you, domina," he whispered. He gulped down his wine. I took only a sip. I almost vomited. "Ah, you've just arrived in Greece," said the old slave. "Many Romans can't stomach our resinated wine."

It was true. It was all very well to hear Petronius Arbiter extol the glories of Hellenic culture, but it was quite another thing to imbibe revolting wine while being relegated to the indoors because of my gender.

"I'm not going to spend my time in Greece playing this ridiculous role," I said. "Even Hylas has more freedom that I do."

"He has," said Hector, "until some treacherous servant decides to poison you. Then he'll be put to death, too."

Hylas let out a squeal of alarm. But it seemed that the older man was completely indifferent to his fate. Was Aristotle right, that some people were just born to be slaves, that they could not transcend their condition? I could not believe that.

"Are you a Stoic?" I asked him. After all, Epictetus's philosophy had come from Greece.

"Far worse than that, domina," said Hector. "I'm a Chrestianos."

He was beyond my help. They would get around to executing him sooner or later. Of all the deluded cults in the Empire, his was the one least likely to engage people's sympathy. Presently he shuffled away. The other attendants followed him, discreetly leaving me with my body-slave.

"Get some rest, domine," said Hylas. "I've sent everyone away. I'll watch you while you sleep. You haven't healed yet. Please."

"I'm wide awake," I said. "I want to go somewhere."

"It's the middle of the night, domine."

"For the last eleven days," I said, "I've been either in a drugged oblivion, or desperately trying to send my mind far away to avoid the agony of the Divinity's *ars amatoria*. While Himself is away for the night, I want to be free for an hour. I want to see Corinth."

"As Empress?"

"As *me*."

"You mean —"

"Yes, Hylas. I'll disguise myself. As *myself*."

"But Himself said you must not accompany him as a boy. Here, you must be the Divine Empress."

"I am not going to accompany him. I am going to do what Nero Himself does so many times in Rome ... You and I are going to slip out into the stews of Corinth, Hylas, a pair of nobodies, vicariously enjoying the infamous night life of this city."

Hylas spent an hour carefully scrubbing away the white paint from my face, the dark lines of kohl about my eyes, the rose-tinted lips and cheeks. He found me a clean plain *chiton*. It was in the Ionian style, because I could not wear the Doric, open at the sides; I needed to conceal my less-than-manhood. I made Hylas dress more grandly than me; this time, perhaps, he would seem to be *my* owner.

***

Preparing to go out took us almost until dawn, but I still was not tired. Just one hour of freedom, I thought, one hour of anonymity. When we left through the front door, we weren't noticed. Gallio's slaves were probably too busy worrying about whether they would live or die, and they weren't that familiar with what I looked like. In Roman society, what you wear identifies you as much as many facial features.

We giggled like children as we left the villa behind us. Though this was a strange city, it was not cluttered and labyrinthine like Rome. The real Corinth was long gone, from a series of civil wars; Julius Caesar's recreation of Corinth was strictly according to the Roman colonial template: here the temples, over there the theater, here again a forum.

But I felt like a boy again, giddy with short-term freedom, running down an alley with a playmate. I had not felt this way for a long time. The unimaginative architecture was not my concern. We raced down an alley, rounded a temple, startled a dove-seller as he hawked sacrificial birds in cages in front of the Temple of Octavia.

We laughed as he chased the birds, hopping along the steps.

"Let's help him," I said to Hylas.

We bent down and started to catch the birds. They seemed tame, not wanting to fly away.

I realized their wings were clipped.

I handed a bird to the vendor, and he sighed as he returned it to the cage. "Yes, I know," he said. "It saves time."

"It seems a pity," I said. "Birds should fly." I thought of my own fate.

"In my country," he said in a strange accent, "the buyers don't wring their necks to honor the gods. In fact, they set them free, to earn merit in their next life."

"That is a beautiful idea."

"But what the clients don't know is … their wings are clipped anyway. I was a bird-seller's slave once. My job was to catch the escaped birds so we could sell them again. The clients did not know the birds were used again and again, so their intentions were pure."

"It seems less wasteful than killing them," I said.

"If me was a bird," Hylas said — his Greek had not yet caught up with his Latin — "Me rather die than not fly."

"What country are you from?" I asked him.

"I'm from the very farthest limit of the Hellenic

world," said the vendor, "beyond even the Empire of Caesar. "I am from Bactria, which is in India."

"The farthest footfall of Alexander the Great," I said, remembering some past comment of my tutor Aristarchos.

"You've heard of it! My, you had a good tutor," he said. "You are not who you seem to be, young master." We finished caging the birds and the vendor handed us an *obol* for our efforts. "Go share a lamb skewer."

We left the temple steps and turned another corner. The sun was rising. I could smell grilled spiced meat and warm bread, and I could tell we were near a market. "You heard him," Hylas said in Latin. "Lamb."

"You go." I had become despondent suddenly. I could not help thinking of the flightless doves, captured and recaptured to ease the sensibilities of pilgrims.

Damnatio Memoriae · 32

V

THE RING OF THE DEATH-GOD

I did not feel I could eat anything, but Hylas was happy to eat a skewer he purchased, along with a flatbread, for our *obol*. And just like that, we were penniless again, but I was content to breathe in the smells and bask in the cacophony of the market coming to life at dawn.

But this is the strange thing: there were virtually no women. The few I saw were veiled and accompanied by a chaperone or a slave. It wasn't as though women were not allowed out of the house; more that well brought up women didn't go out. You'd see an old crone buying vegetables, or a little girl.

In Rome, women are *seen*. They make a point of it. They may not have many rights by law, but Rome is full of powerful women pulling strings behind the scenes. I had known many. In a sense, I *was* one of them, brought back to life and inhabiting the corpus of an ex-delicatus.

Here in the agora, women were all but invisible. But there were men everywhere. Men of all ages, eating, arguing, playing games. As we passed by, they would whistle at us, blow kisses in the air, ask our names. It was quite brazen — it is odd, but you don't get this in Rome, the city of scandal and excess. In Rome it is grossly indecent to proposition a freeborn boy. Why would you, when there are slaves who must submit to any depraved whim?

We minded our own business, ignored the suggestive comments. We played hide and seek behind the market stalls. We pilfered vegetables. We ran. We laughed a lot. And then ...

I spotted the ring.

Rather, Hylas tripped me, and I skidded past the stalls and into a pile of costly fabrics. And my eye came level with a silver platter that held this ring. The stone was just a handspan from my eye. It was a large carnelian intaglio and it showed Proserpina (Persephone as the Greeks call her) in a field of grain. Behind her, cape flying, the God of Death was bearing down, about to seize the beautiful goddess and carry her down to the underworld. Somehow, in infinitesimal detail, the eyes were so cunningly carved that they seemed to stare right back at me. So tiny, yet the image drew me into its blood-tinged depths. I could hear Persephone cry out in ecstasy and terror.

A voice whispered in my ear ... my secret name, known only to the one person who spoke my language, who was now dead. I froze. I felt the breath of Hyacinth, a gust from the dark caves of the dead. The image carved into pink stone drew me into its world. I recognized it. Hyacinth's spirit must have led me here.

All at once I was reliving the dream that haunted me as I lay in pain on the voyage. I had seen Nero and Poppaea as the King and Queen of the Underworld.

Without thinking, I picked up the ring.

"Thief!" someone was shouting.

I stood there, holding the ring, staring into it, oblivious to the stir I was creating. We were not in one of the market stalls but a shop that bordered on the agora. The fabrics were on display on tables in front of the entrance. A bearded man was scowling at me. "Think you're just going to walk off with it?"

"No, no," I stuttered. "I'll buy it."

"Impertinent urchin!" he said, and began to rain down blows on me with his fists. "'I'll buy it' indeed! This ring is worth a dozen of you."

At that moment, the street filled with Roman soldiers. Two of them seized the proprietor and shoved him roughly against a column. "Why are you pushing me around? It's that thieving boy you should be punishing."

"I told you I would buy it!" I said hotly.

"With what?"

Croesus was making his way through the small mob that had gathered around us. He held out a pouch of coins. He threw it at the shop owner, who, still restrained by soldiers, could not pick it up.

One of the soldiers did, opened it, and took one of the coins out. It was a shiny, newly minted aureus.

"You struck a member of the Imperial family," he said. "That's a summary crucifixion."

In that moment, my status abruptly shifted. I went from invisible boy to the center of attention. A crowd was gathering ... though they kept their distance. Though Greece was the pride of Rome, it was also a conquered nation. I watched the vendor's face. He had been so certain of his place, of who he was, of what I was. Now his world was chaos.

"I — I didn't how. How could I know? Look at how these boys are dressed!"

A soldier struck him in the face. "You're making it worse."

Then that soldier went down on one knee in front of me. "I'm sorry you were bothered, Divinitas," he said. "We'll take it from here."

I had not been free for a single moment. My carefree games with my slave, gathering up the lame doves, playing hide and seek among the merchant stalls ... all of it had been carefully, discreetly observed. They had been ready to swoop in at any moment.

"Let the man go," I said. "He couldn't have known."

The vendor fell to his knees, slobbered over my sandals. "Forgive me." He added, "Please keep the ring! No need for any payment. Just spare me the cross."

The Romans certainly understood the effectiveness of a good deterrent. That was how they kept the world subjugated. How *we* kept it so, I reminded myself, for I too was one of the oppressors now.

They were going to lead him away, but I held my hand up. "No, no, I'm serious. He can go. And give him his money." The gesture of magnanimity felt empty. Even as I ordered his release, I knew that I would not always be able to act this way. Sometimes, to show mercy would be to seem weak, or worse still, would seem to contradict the will of the Divine Nero; that could never be allowed. But the God was not watching.

"You would do well to remember the tale of Philemon and Baucis, who knew how to serve the god even when he was disguised as an impoverished wanderer," Croesus said. "And you, my Empress," he added, "must be properly escorted back to the mansion."

Croesus waved and a magnificent litter appeared.

"I'm not going back to the mansion," I said.

"But, Divinitas —"

"Croesus, you see how I am dressed. Don't treat me like a woman. I won't be sequestered. Later I'll put on a veil and be chaste and demure, but right now, I want to go to the house of Thaïs the *hetaira*."

I knew what I needed to do with the ring.

"Divinitas!" Croesus said.

"You know you have to obey me," I said. "Everyone does. Except *Him*." It was only in that moment that I understood how much power I had. And that I relished that power, even as it made me feel queasy to use it.

"Hylas!" I hissed. The illusion of equality vanished in an instant. My body slave crouched down by the litter so I could step in on his back. I stomped up, knowingly hurting him a little. He clambered in after me and drew the curtain.

"Thank you, domine, for letting me feel free for a moment," Hylas said, and kissed my hand.

In the privacy of the litter, as we bounced through the streets of Corinth, I started to embrace him. But the gulf between us could no longer be breached. I knew that, even though we had played at being children together, slipping into the city past the prying eyes of the staff and the guards, Hylas had found a way to alert them. He had understood, far sooner than I, how the world I now inhabited really worked.

"There is only one way we can really be friends," I said to him. "I'll have to free you."

"Don't," he said softly. "Please don't."

Damnatio Memoriae · 38

VI

THE HOUSE OF THE HETAIRA

Oh, the ring! The ill-fated, infamous ring that you gave Nero as a wedding present! The ring that is now seen as the prophecy of your fate!

Yes. It's because of that ring that I have been condemned to take the same pathway to the underworld as Persephone, Queen of the Dead.

But what of it? Vitellius would have decreed some other death for me, something just as grotesque, would he not?

If you had known, would it have been your choice of wedding gift?

What is the use of speculating?

If I had known, I would have hidden myself more carefully in the forest, and I would never have been captured and sold. Don't you think I haven't thought about all the *what ifs* and *what if nots*?

If I had hidden in the forest and crawled back into the village once they had done all their looting, there would have been no one left. They took everything. They killed everyone they didn't enslave. I'd have been reduced to some kind of feral existence. Or tried to find my way to the next village, and who's to say they wouldn't sell me themselves, a child with no relatives, good for a quick few denarii?

So … I don't put any stock in the ring's ill omens. Something else would have happened. Life is one long misery, flecked with the occasional fleeting moment of joy.

And how did you come to give the ring to Himself?

I was getting to that.

***

I had expected that the *hetaira* would inhabit some sleazy lupanar like the ones I'd seen in Rome, where you go in and pay an old woman and make your selection from a roomful of preening prostitutes. But we arrived in a tasteful villa on the outskirts of Corinth.

In a colonnaded porch, the Emperor's Praetorians stood at attention, as they probably had been the whole night. The soldiers who had accompanied me joined them; most of my entourage from my lodgings had gone back, leaving me only with Hylas. The soldiers exchanged words, but none prevented me from entering.

There was a foyer beyond the porch, with a floor mosaic in a nondescript geometric design; the walls, too, were plain with only a touch of gold in the molding. Beyond the porch was a little courtyard; to the left a peristyle whose only decoration was a breathtaking statue of Aphrodite embracing her son Eros, so vividly painted it almost seemed they breathed.

I knew then that *this* was the Greece Rome tried, in its overblown way, to emulate. This was the Greece I recognized from the classical proportions of Petronius's villa — nothing in excess, a few art objects, and each one exquisite and unique.

Sounds were coming from a neighboring room. Not the shrieks and cackles of a Roman party, but a kind of murmuring, like the sea. I could hear the plangent keening of a double flute, the paired notes intertwining in alternating consonance and discord. Then the mournful twang of a *kithara*. And the voice of a singer.

As I entered the room, Hylas shadowing me, the song was ending. It was in fact one of the famous soliloquies from *The Myrmidons* by Aeschylus:

Kai men, philó gar, abdelykt' emoi tade...
And yet to me, it is not loathsome, because I love him.

The singer sang the phrase *philó gar* over and over, caressing each note as it hovered in the air, punctuated by the *kithara* and melding into the sobbing *aulos*. I recognized him: it was none other than Lucius Domitius Paris, the renowned singer whose techniques Himself often tried to emulate.

It was a select group, no more than a dozen, and I did not know any of the others except my husband, who did not sit enthroned but shared a couch with the *hetaira*. I assumed that was who it was because she was the only woman in the room.

Thaïs was no painted whore. She wore less makeup than most of the men. She was simply dressed, though it was expensive simplicity.

No one could see me yet; the lamps were on the drinking-table, and the doorway was in shadow.

Thaïs spoke — and all the men listened. "You can see," she said, "what Aeschylus means when he gives Achilles those words to say. He's telling us we are beautiful because we are loved. Beauty is not intrinsic."

"Surely," Paris said, "Achilles is speaking here about the mangled corpse of Patroclus. No verbal acrobatics could render beautiful a dead man covered in blood."

"No acrobatics?" said a little man, wedged between two large ones, sitting on the right couch. "You have given us verbal acrobatics aplenty!"

"Indeed, Strato," said the Emperor. "Paris has outdone himself. He portrayed both the hideous spectacle and the redeeming love with just a few modulated tones. But was it feeling? Or was it merely technique?"

"Both, I should hope," Thaïs said, laughing.

"Do you have a better poem, Strato?" said Paris. "We've all heard that when it comes to writing about the boys, you have no peer."

Strato rose and came to the front of the table. He was about to launch into some ditty when, I suppose, he noticed me.

"Sometimes," he said, "words fail me, when one such as *this* enters the room."

Himself, the Divine Nero, Master of the World, saw me at last, for I had stepped into the light.

"I told you stay at home," he said. A hint of menace in his voice.

"Poppaea's home," I said softly. "I am Sporus."

"Oh ... of course," said the Emperor. Had I confused him? "My wife," he said, "the Divine Poppaea Sabina, is indeed back at the villa, sitting demurely at her loom no doubt, and on her best Greek behavior. Perhaps, like

Penelope, she's weaving a tapestry to celebrate my return from this symposium. But this, friends, is my one true love … my *eromenos*."

"What?" Thaïs said. "Am I not lover enough for you, my Emperor?" She beckoned me to come closer. "Though it's good to see you adopt our customs, Divinitas." She looked at me for a long time and finally she exclaimed, "*O pais kalós*! Is such beauty even possible?"

She made me come a little closer and continued, "If I were Poppaea, I'd have had you killed by now."

The tension was almost intolerable. My boldness in coming here seemed like a mistake. Could Thaïs see through me? Did she know what a tightrope I was walking? Everyone was silent. With Nero, you never knew when an outburst might occur. I steeled myself for his wrath.

Suddenly —

"I have a poem," Strato announced. And he began to recite:

O you are fair, young Sporus, and ripe for love;
 But even if you marry, we won't leave you alone.

There was a burst of applause.

This was not the time to imitate Poppaea … or rather, to imitate the *idea* of Poppaea, as the aloof, cloistered Empress. The way to brazen this out would be to act more male than I had ever acted during my time in Rome. This was a different world. A boy was not a painted plaything here. I had to suppress my feelings of victimhood, for the myths and histories that Aristarchos had used to teach me Greek were beginning to feel real. In this society, lovers fought and died together, made vows to each other that were as important to society as those between man and wife, gave their lives for each other.

In this world, I could be celebrated and honored as Nero's boy ... and feel fully male. A supreme irony, since strangers had tossed my maleness onto some Roman rubbish heap.

I strode up to the man who had treated me as a rag to wipe off the detritus of his own emotional conflicts. Laughing, I launched myself onto his lap, fully expecting to be slapped for my impertinence.

He was nonplussed for only a moment. Then he too laughed, hugged me, and kissed me, rather chastely and decorously, on the lips.

And whispered, too low for anyone to hear: "Well played, Sporus. I can see there's no keeping you locked away. Well, when we're with friends, we can do as they do. But when I need it, you *will* be Poppaea."

"Yes, Lucius," I said, smiling sweetly. He was the most powerful man in the world, but there were things I could hold over him. "In any case, my Lord," I added, "I saw something in the market I thought you'd like, and I hurried to make you a gift of it."

I motioned for Hylas to come and kneel at the Emperor's feet. He held up the box with the ring with the intaglio of the Queen of the Dead.

Himself took the ring and held it up to his eye, admiring the detail.

"It's to celebrate our wedding," I said.

"The Rape of Persephone!" said the Emperor, his brow darkening. "Is this what you think of me?"

Strato, the silly poet, gasped. Thaïs raised an eyebrow.

It was only in that moment that I realized what an ill omen it was.

VII

Two Lives

It was in that instant that my double life in Greece began. The Emperor, it would seem, was to be accompanied on his grand tour by both Empress and *Eromenos*. Of course, they would never be seen at the same event. That would be most distasteful. Disrespectful to the wife, to flaunt the lover to her face.

Not to mention the logistics of switching identities — including clothes and makeup — in the blink of an eye. Though, since proper women weren't seen in public much, and usually veiled, I did manage to transform from time to time, when the Divinitas needed it.

But I was speaking of the omen.

The Divine Caesar was still glowering, and the guests were fidgeting. "Are you saying that you are the innocent maiden, and that I am the rapacious God of Death? After all I've done for you?"

Casually, he kicked Hylas out of the way. The boy suppressed a whimper. He did not want to compound the situation.

I had to think on my feet. "Persephone was already a goddess," I said, "and the daughter of a goddess. I was nothing before you set your eyes on me."

"Not so," said Nero. "You were the God Hymen, watching over me during a drunken wedding."

That had been the first time I ever set eyes on Himself. Yet I had not known until this moment that the Divine Nero had known the whole time that *I* was the hallucination of the God. It meant he had been watching me for longer than I knew. It meant that I had lost my freedom long before I knew I had freedom to lose.

Nero pulled me onto his lap. He stroked my hair. His expression was unreadable, even to me. It was Thaïs who came to my rescue.

"The beautiful boy is only a barbarian," she said, her voice soothing. "He can't be expected to understand our complex philosophies."

"Yes. A barbarian. That's right," I said. I tried to kiss the Emperor, but he turned his head; I caught a chinful of wine, perfume, and vomit. "That's why the Empress suffers me to live," I went on. "I'm just a pretty face. I can't speak of philosophy or poetry."

Nero seemed satisfied with how I had finessed the situation. Still stroking my hair, he spoke, softly so none could hear: "Later, we'll discuss this." I pretended not to notice the tone of menace.

Meanwhile, the *hetaira* Thaïs started to stroke my hair as well. She whispered in my other ear: "Your secret is safe, dear. People like you and me, we know how to survive." But which of my many secrets did she know?

She and the Emperor embraced, with me trapped between them, being squashed like a pillow. If you could imagine the combined scents: the clashing perfumes, the many wines, the viands and stomach fluids ... all of them battering my nose while I tried not to gasp for air ...

At length, they pulled apart. It then pleased the Divinitas to feed me personally. The food was not extravagant, not like back home; there were no peacocks' brains. But the grapes were as sweet as any I had ever tasted.

At length, a weariness came over the Emperor, and he nodded off quite suddenly, like a lamp that has run out of fuel.

"Leave him be for a few hours," Thaïs said. "Would you care to see my domain?"

She motioned to the flute-players, who struck up a lullaby. I looked around and saw that most of the guests were visibly more at ease, and some, like the poet Strato, were drifting off as well.

She took my hand and led me through the peristyle to a hidden stairway to an upper floor. Again, pure simplicity. A hallway and some doorways. The floor was plain wood, but beautifully polished.

"What were you expecting, my beautiful boy? Lewd ladies pouting in the corridor?"

"It's not what I've seen in Rome," I said.

"In Rome, men and women dine together," she said. "Here, a proper woman is never seen unveiled. But men long for a woman they can be themselves with. Not just discuss art and music. Just not to feel awkward. People like me are very special, you see. We can stroke their egos *and* their organs!"

"But what about power?" I said. "In Rome, women run *everything*. Though no one admits it."

"And you don't think that's true here?" She laughed, and then showed me a door that was slightly ajar. She pushed it a little way and I saw a man lying with his eyes closed, being tended to by a younger *hetaira*. Seeing her mistress, the girl was about to speak, but Thaïs put a finger to her lips.

"Isn't that ..." I whispered ... "General Titus Flavius Vespasianus?"

Even in the dim light from a single oil lamp, I remembered the general all right. He had gazed at me with an unnerving concupiscence the day he had come to get his marching orders for Judaea. And Statilia herself had told me he was rumored to be in the running for the next Divinitas.

"Why isn't he at the symposium?" I said softly.

"It would spoil the surprise," Vespasian said, with his eyes still closed. Then he added, in that growl affected by military commanders, "The Emperor's bumboy! I'd know those dulcet tones anywhere. Well, Sporus, I am glad to make your acquaintance again. Thaïs, you may as well send the girl away."

"I'd better leave," I said.

"Ah, come, boy, not quite yet," said the general, sitting up and patting his sweaty paunch. Again, he stared at me like some sweetmeat on a platter.

"I thought you were off slaughtering Jews," I said.

"I'll be slaughtering them soon enough," he said. "They're too stubborn to behave like a proper colony. I might even have to raze their capital city to the ground and enslave the entire population. Nero's express orders. But you think I enjoy being the villain? So ... I thought I'd stop off on the way and visit the Olympics; I hear Caesar is competing himself."

"It's the wrong year," I teased, knowing that Nero had had the Olympiad calendar rewritten for his own convenience.

"Time means nothing to the gods," he said. "Come and rub my back, there's a good lad."

"I'm not a whore," I said.

I left quickly, slamming the door a little bit too loudly.

"Well played," the *hetaira* said, smiling a little. "He won't forget you if he comes to power."

"I wasn't playing," I said.

"That's the very of art of it," Thaïs said. "I am the most famous courtesan in Corinth, and you outclass me utterly."

"I'm a boy," I said. "I can be direct."

"The trick, then," said Thaïs, "is to do it as Empress. Oh, don't panic, I know. I've always known."

I must have stared at her openmouthed. She embraced me and said, "We're going to be friends, Sporus."

VIII

ELEUSIS

The next day, Himself the Divine Nero and his Imperial Consort — that is to say, my castrated self — sat in state in the villa of the disgraced proconsul and were duly paid court to by the important personalities of Corinth.

The traditional *Salutatio* takes place every morning. After my patronus's death, I myself had presided sometimes. But not in the palace. The morning petitions were a public matter, but the Divinitas's cubiculum capers were not, though I understand that in Caligula's time, things were done a lot less by the ironclad rules of tradition. But now, I was Empress. I sat right next to the Divine Nero, though discreetly veiled so as not to scandalize the natives. Thus it was that we attempted to accommodate the excesses of Roman life to the classicism of the Hellenes.

I was made to fit into every world, though I belonged to none of them.

Thaïs, of course, did not come; such women are not

guests in respectable homes in Greece.

It was a desultory scene. For one thing, the Emperor was — by his own way of thinking — travelling incognito. Just one ship, and without the cacophonous circus of hundreds of retainers. Even though the whole city knew that Nero was there, they had all been strongly cautioned that he did not wish to cause a stir.

There was only a handful of petitioners as we held court. It pleased the Divinitas to dispense justice in person. Some land disputes, an argument over a tutor violating the honor of some highborn youth, and a forger who was so arrogant nobody much minded when the Emperor sentenced him to having his hands cut off and hung around his neck. This was done discreetly, off-stage, like violence in a Greek tragedy, and it was just as well that our prandium was not marred by bloodshed.

It was time to go to Eleusis, the place of supreme mystery, the place of the soul's rebirth. I was to be carried there with great honor, as Empress and Goddess, with no outsiders allowed to see my face.

***

To do so we would enter Athens by night, but we would not have time to enjoy the sights, for at dawn, we each had to sacrifice a piglet before setting off on the pilgrimage on foot.

We had come humbly, with virtually no retinue. A small military escort, naturally, with General Vespasian taking command himself, though I was not sure if he was there out of loyalty to the Emperor or to keep an eye on my frayed beauty. Hovering about were the usual poets and poetasters with whom Nero loved to surround himself, including the actor Paris and the poet Strato who so seemed to admire the boys. In addition, there came my slave Hylas, and Croesus, who was able to give a kind of running commentary, explaining the curious goings-on to me.

To the Divinitas as well, for the Divine Nero preferred the lurid bits of Greek literature and had not really studied as much philosophy as he wanted others to believe. But he could not be seen to be requesting any elucidations, so eavesdropping on his emptyheaded little Empress was a good way to acquire any necessary tidbits.

The basic story, of course, I knew; we had a similar one in my country, though the names were all different. Persephone in the fields where flowers of Tyrian purple bloomed, in the full beauty of young maidenhood; Hades bursting up from Hell and dragging her to the murky depths of the kingdom of the dead; Ceres scouring the world, cursing it with eternal winter in grief; the six pomegranate seeds that meant six months of cold and six of warmth, birthing the circle of time.

What Croesus told us, though, I did not know.

He told us that we ourselves would die and be reborn in the sacred mysteries.

"Oh," I said, "like the Christianoi."

For I remembered that that wayward sect too had among its strange doctrines some surprisingly normal-sounding ones, including the self-sacrificing god who dies in the spring to fertilize the world with his divine blood, and then returns to life after three days.

"Not like them," said Croesus, "or any other divine resurrection cult. In the mysteries, you will *actually* die and be reborn."

"Metaphorically," said the Emperor.

"Begging your Divinity's pardon," Croesus said, "I do

believe we are speaking in literal terms."

"Oh, nonsense," said Nero. "I've killed thousands of people. They don't come back, you know. But their longing remains. And you can feed on that longing. That's what we eat, you know. What sustains our immortality. Every pinprick life is a part of our forever."

We who? I thought. *We gods?*

As always, the Divinitas stood right on the line that divides the visionary from the lunatic.

The procession moved slowly, with those seeking initiation pausing every few hours often to pray or sacrifice. As the night wore on, others paused to rest, but our party marched through the darkness, having changed the bearers at sunset.

***

We arrived, then, ahead of the rest of the party, which was not really in the spirit of the pilgrimage. And it was clear that Eleusis might have seen better days. The winding road to the temple was lined with hawkers of souvenirs who were just setting up their wares, expecting a crowd at dawn: ill-favored statues of Demeter, tawdry jewelry, and crude versions of the ring I had presented to the Divinitas. There were images in the ancient style, angular and not natural-looking. There were piglets stacked dozens to a cage, waiting to be sacrificed.

I saw little, though I heard, and smelled, a great deal. I had to peer through a slit in the drapes of the litter; for I was traveling in public, demurely veiled, invisible and inviolable to men.

The portico of the temple was unattended. The procession was exactly timed by age-old tradition; no one was expected to have forged on ahead. I sent Croesus to roust up some kind of reception. There were steps that led up to the temple proper. There was a colonnade of simple Doric columns. It was dark, not yet dawn; light came from two torches burning in braziers on either side of a worn, oak door. So this was the sanctuary, the home of the great mystery of death and rebirth, the place from which you could descend into the very bowels of Erebus.

Eventually, a bearded priest emerged, still straightening his *himation*, followed by a young novice rubbing his eyes. Perhaps they had been rehearsing for the fertility rites.

Clearing his throat, in a tone of practiced arrogance, the priest said, "Who art thou? Whence comest thou, and what dost thou seek?"

"I should think that would be pretty obvious," said the Divinitas.

I whispered in his ear.

"I am a child of Earth and Starry Heaven," said the Divinitas.

"I think that comes later in the ritual," I said.

"Will the Empress be participating with the women?" said the priest, and I noticed a rather brawny priestess standing in the distance, staring at me like a lioness in the circus.

"I'll go as *eromenos*," I said quickly, for I did not want to be split from our company; however strange we were, we were familiar to one another.

I pulled the curtain aside. I stepped from the litter. I threw down my veil, ripped away my purple stola, and stood there in a plain tunica, to all who looked upon me an intact boy.

The novice giggled, and the high priest turned around

and slapped him.

"You don't say anything," said Nero, "and the sanctity of this place will be upheld and respected by Rome."

"Yes, Divinitas," said the high priest. And he knelt at the feet of the Living God.

The boy beckoned to us. He winked at me and had an impertinent, knowing grin. Perhaps he too had acquired his position in society by dint of talents other than religious.

The high priest opened the door.

As we set foot in that most hallowed place, the Divine Nero whispered in my ear: "This place," he said, "is shit."

He said it in Latin, so the Greeks pretended they had not heard.

IX

Mysteries of Life and Death

Turning at the doorway, I saw that the procession that had set out along the sacred way was only now beginning to catch up. As the sun rose, I saw a line of celebrants waving branches.

"We need not wait for them," said the high priest. "The Divinitas has, as I understand it, requested a private initiation."

He shut the door. Only the Divine Nero and I had been allowed to step through. Even our slaves remained outside.

I heard faint chanting from the suppliants outside.

"Come," said the priest. "You will stand in the Telesterion, hall of the gods, built when the world was new."

We crossed the hallway, and we were in an area open to the sky, though surrounded by colonnades. Bathed in the light of dawn were heaps of rubble. We reached what may have once been a vast chamber, now roofless. There were broken columns wreathed in vines. This was once a temple, and I could well believe it existed at the dawn of history, when the gods of Olympus still dined with kings. A pungent aroma suffused the air.

Against a far wall, a few people were scurrying about. They looked up at us, seemingly surprised to be caught. They had masks. They were half-dressed. They were perhaps actors, part of the reenactment of the story of Persephone that was to come. The priest waved them away, mouthing "Not yet!" Then he turned back to us.

"This is the show?" said the Divine Emperor. "It's like a slow day at the Circus."

"I am the High Hierophant of the Temple of Demeter. Be humble," said the priest. "For soon you will meet the gods."

"Good," said the Emperor. "I've never met an equal before."

Nero was showing the kind of bravado that only emerged when something was unnerving him. I had seen him at his most vulnerable. I knew.

Another young acolyte entered bearing a worn red-figure *kylix* filled with a strange frothing fluid.

"Drink," said the priest. "This is *kykeon*, the nectar that opens the gateway to the other world."

The Emperor seized the bowl and drank, then handed me the dregs. The liquid was bitter.

"More," said the Master of the World.

"Divinitas," said the priest, "the dose is mostly carefully gauged. There could be danger. You could be lost in the other world, never to emerge again."

Nero scoffed. "But that is a dosage for mortals. And I

need to go farther. Beyond where mortals go. So does my Empress."

"Today, my Lord," I said, for I feared being lost in a labyrinth of the mind, "I am only your *eromenos*."

"Words," said Nero, "are only labels. We shall use whatever labels we like, and they shall mean whatever we say they mean. Let's have some more of this magic potion of yours."

The acolyte motioned and another, almost a twin, emerged with a small amphora of the potion. He refilled the *kylix*. I sipped at it. My Divine Husband took the entire amphora, threw his head back, and began pouring.

"Lucius —" I whispered.

"This isn't Rome," he said. "The senate's not hiding behind every pillar, hunched under my bed, waiting to catch my every faux pas. I'm in Greece, the gods' home country. Here I am as free as any other god."

He clutched my free hand. He was trembling. Something was taking hold of him, something different from his mercurial mood changes. Was it the hallucinatory posset? Or was it his own mind, that mad mix of power and insecurities? I held on to him, steadying him. I put back the smaller *kylix*. I reached out with my other hand and stroked his back, feeling both tenderness and stark terror.

"Come with me!" he whispered harshly. "I can't go in there alone!"

Terror overtook tenderness. He pushed the amphora against my lips. I took a gulp and then he quaffed it to the dregs and flung it so it smashed, smashed against smashed marble. The Emperor gripped my hand and then stepped ... *somewhere*.

He was still there, of course. But somehow, he was

not. He had left his body. Where he had been there was a bodily vessel, but it was empty, as though it had been molded form a pile of papyrus. My mind was awhirl, but I was still in the real world. I willed myself to follow …

Around me, walls of fire. No sky. Only a limitless, unbroken gray.

"Lucius!" I cried out …

Figures wavered. Were they the King and Queen of the Underworld? Smoke rose up. I was choking from an acrid, unfamiliar odor. The King leered at me, his eyes wild.

"Lucius!" I cried again …

***

You are silent. I want to hear more.

He's here! How did you manage it? He's standing before me, in a dressing room in the Circus Maximus, looking at me with the same eyes. His face … his face is like the night.

I've done a masterful job, then. Why, this is the slave, brought all the way to Rome from the markets of Carthage, captured somewhere in some dark forest beyond the desert that borders the southern limit of the Empire … rather like you, Sporus … a creature from the edge of the world. I used all my art to transform him into our Greek and Roman Lord of the Dead Lands.

This is the man who will kill me? He is as dark as I am pale. What kind of metaphor are the organizers aiming for?

Why not introduce the two of you? It wouldn't do to die at the hand of a stranger. Did I say hand? But you know what organ I meant.

I was talking about a religious experience. And you

parade this creature before me — my executioner?

It will be a sweet execution for him. But he'll be following you to the dark country. He is scheduled to be eaten by crocodiles afterward.

He doesn't seem unhappy.

He doesn't understand a word of Latin ... or Greek, for that matter. My dominus picked him out from a lot that were about to go off to a latifundia, to be worked to death. He knows nothing of any of this. He's just happily living from meal to meal. And you'll be his nicest. As befits being his last.

And now you expect me to speak of the mysteries of life and death?

I'll leave you two to get to know each other. Audiences like it when their stars have relationships that go beyond what they see in the arena. The performances are more moving, more multi-layered.

Performances? This creature is no performer. They've picked the most monstrous executioner of all, twice my height, a mass of muscle. And yet I imagine that the Emperor Nero might have accounted him beautiful. After all, Aeschylus calls the God of Death *nekrodegmon*, entertainer of the dead.

I'm sure our friend is very much moved by the words of four-hundred-year-old poets.

***

Yes, I saw Death.

I looked Death in the eye.

Death was a hulking, dark, monster of a man. Death was not a god at all.

There in the Temple of Demeter, Death loomed above me, blotting out the rising sun. The priests and novices were performing a masked play, reenacting the ancient myth, but the Death in my vision was mine alone.

My Death.

The Emperor stood alone too, lost in his own private vision. In his imagination, was I with him as the mythic drama unfolded, as he conversed with Olympians? When Ganymede poured his wine at the banquet of the immortals, did he have my face?

I know I saw Death.

And now, looking into the eyes of the slave who will ravish me to death, I see now that it was a premonition.

The Emperor and I were not sharing a journey into the heart of the underworld. But I believe that he thought I was with him. This entire experience, this communal death and rebirth, was a lie. The magic potion was a delusion. In my vision, I was alone.

X

Olympia

Indeed, Himself did not tell me much about the experience we had supposedly shared. He probably assumed I experienced it as well. Over the ensuing days hints about it would spring from his lips at odd moments, sometimes while he slept.

The journey to Olympia was a slow triumphal progress, as though the Divinitas had already been awarded the laurels of the victor. It was also — despite the fact that all of the Greek world had been integrated into Rome for generations — carried out with all the trappings of conquest, with the military advancing before and after.

We moved slowly, the soldiers tramping at a ceremonial pace, sitting on a palanquin as large as a cubiculum, borne by two dozen matched slaves. Even the slaves wore purple, more precious than gold.

At each stop, there were crowds, sometimes with petitions, sometimes just there to gawk at the Living God and his perfect boy — or, sometimes, his demurely veiled Empress. More and more, I became adept at whatever role I was assigned, transforming daily, even hourly. For I was never more a slave than when I was a freedman. It was magic. A dab of kohl, a daub of red, a subtle change to the blended perfumes, and I *was* the Goddess Poppaea, materializing from beyond the grave.

On our progress, stately villas of the wealthy were opened up, and our party swarmed through them like locusts.

Though they had conquered Rome with their culture, these were still a conquered people. The ostentatious estates were the country homes of Roman senators, not of Greeks.

"The rich Greeks," Croesus told me, "have all moved to Alexandria."

***

And yet ... Olympia.

Olympia was well maintained. Gleaming. Rome had added to its structures but kept its classic lines. Olympia was how one imagines Greece. Gleaming columns surrounded a palaestra where youths were wrestling.

I was foolish enough to ask Croesus where Mt. Olympus was.

"Olympia is nowhere near Olympus," he said, suppressing a smile.

But the Emperor said, "Don't make fun of him. He's an innocent, a tabula rasa. A perfect being to receive all my wisdom, and more besides."

I was tiring of the double entendres. But then again, I was in and of myself a double creature, wasn't I?

Our party had come to rest just in front of the Temple of Zeus, which was to be, despite how far I'd come since being captured by pirates and sold, the first time I ever laid eyes on one of the Seven Wonders of the World.

"Come," said the Divinitas, tugging my arm. "I want you to meet my celestial counterpart."

Quickly, up the steps, ignoring the hangers-on, I was pushed into a sacred place for the second time. The Temple of Zeus was no derelict ruin, though. The space was awash in light, for gaps in the ceiling let in the sun which was blindingly mirrored in the huge pool of olive oil upon which stood the plinth that held the thirty-cubit-tall statue of Zeus, so towering that even the figure of winged Nike he held in one hand was twice the size of a human being.

Zeus was all ivory and gold. I could not imagine how many elephants had sacrificed their tusks to create a seated deity eight times a man's height. Zeus's *himation* was gold over glass. His brows were furrowed and his eyes bluer than mine. His skin had been subtly painted; not quite a flesh tone, because the creamy white of the ivory still shone through. His skin glistened; attendants anointed him constantly with olive oil, which slowly dripped into a marble-fringed pool.

I felt the god's gaze even before I looked up. And when I did, I could not look away. His eyes held me utterly.

Most temples inspire awe with clouds of incense. Everything is dark and you're on the verge of choking on the bittersweet fragrance. The temple of Zeus was different.

"Look, Sporus," said the Emperor. "There you are!"

I snapped out of my reverie and the Divinitas tugged me forward by the hand again. The Living God was pointing at the Sky God's left foot. He was excited, like a young boy. There was a relief of a boy sculpted on the heel. It could barely be seen in the shadows of the fold of sculpted cloth. The boy held a laurel wreath and was crowning himself.

"It's you," said the Emperor.

By now, there were others in the temple, standing far off; they were members of our own party. And there was a priest, dressed exactly as Zeus was; though he was an old man, he had the sculpted god's impressive musculature; he must have been beautiful as a young man. The priest said, "Few notice that little fellow in relief. It's Pantarkes, who won the boys' wrestling match at the eighty-sixth Olympiad. Four hundred years ago. He was the *eromenos* of the sculptor Pheidias, who immortalized him. You have, indeed, the eyesight of a god, to spot the boy from here."

"Don't I, though!" said Nero, and beamed. The priest seemed to have divined the best way to ingratiate himself with Himself — just casually slip into the conversation that one was aware of his divine nature.

"If you will glance way up there," said the priest, "at the god's fingertip, you'll see the words the sculptor etched."

"Oh, indeed," said the Emperor, squinting.

"You will of course know what it says."

"Of course," Himself said irritably. "But I think I'll test you on it."

"It says, '*Pantarkes kalos,*'" the priest said.

"I know, I know," said the Emperor. "Pantarkes pulcher est." He pretended to translate it for my benefit. "Now, when am I competing?"

General Vespasian approached us, followed by members of our households. I was relieved to have Hylas close by again.

"This place is as dead as a catacomb," he said. "There don't seem to be any games being prepared at all."

"Well, that won't do," said the Emperor.

"Divinitas," said the priest, "It's actually not an Olympiad year."

"But I gave orders to change the year," said Nero. "Was it not done?"

Titus Vespasianus said, "Orders were sent, Divinitas."

"The immutable will of the gods —" the priest began. He stopped himself. Perhaps too late.

Nero pouted. I knew what the pouting presaged.

The general looked at me. The high priest looked at me. My slave looked at me, and the members of the Emperor's household stole glances. No one looked at Himself, the one who owned all Rome. Not directly. To whom belonged the deadlier gaze? The master of this temple, or the Master of the World?

The humblest slave, the mightiest warrior ... they were looking to *me* to save them from Nero's impending fury.

"Lucius, my dearest," I said softly, "it is we who are to blame for arriving so early. Let's give them a little time to finish their preparations. Meanwhile, we can stay here with our cousin Zeus."

Nero continued to glower. But, as suddenly as they had come, the doom-clouds dissipated.

I looked around at the others. I waved them all away. I, who had come from nothing, could command Rome's most respected general.

The temple cleared almost instantly. Even the priest scurried away.

I stood between my Earthly master and my master on Olympus.

And it was just the three of us, unless you counted Nike in the palm of Jove's hand, and little Pantarkes in relief on his foot.

Himself the Divine Nero spoke to the King of Olympus. "Jupiter," he said, addressing him intimately in Latin instead of Greek, as though he were a close family member — or a slave — "I've often thought about what I'd say to you. I've seen you often enough in the Temple of Jupiter Optimus Maximus. But *this* you, one of the wonders of the world, this really is you, isn't it? So I want to ask you ... where is my mother?"

My heart almost stopped beating.

"Don't tell me she's gone," he said. "Don't tell me I killed her. There is no death. Death is a doorway and we, the gods, have the keys. Don't we? Look! I killed Poppaea. Yet here she is. More beautiful than ever."

He pushed me toward the statue. I was trembling. This had to be wrong. As I stepped forward I transformed, my steps echoing Poppaea's, even my breathing breathier.

"If Poppaea can come back, why not my mother?"

He was shaking his fist.

I reached behind and touched his shoulder, which was shaking with rage. Slowly I stroked his shoulder. "Don't mind him," I whispered. "When we get home, you'll convene a senate and they'll make her a goddess."

"Ha!" he cried. "Anything you can do, I can do too! You shoved Heracles up there among the stars. I'll put my mother there — properly, legally, by an act of the senate!"

"Lucius —" I said.

"You've had your sisters? So have I!" he raved, though I'd never heard of the Divine Nero doing anything like that. Perhaps he was identifying with Emperors of the past, like Caligula.

"Mothers? Sisters? Animals? You gods are nothing but incestuous good-for-nothings! And your much-vaunted Ganymede, the most beautiful youth in the universe? Not a patch on my Sporus. I'll show you!"

With that, Nero ripped my tunica and exposed me in just my subligaculum. All at once I found myself metamorphosing into my boy persona. Even though I had been on display many times, at banquets or in the baths, I never felt so humiliated, even though my only audience was a statue. This was not Petronius, proud of my beauty, trying to get his poet friends to write verses about my smooth limbs and lovely eyes. "Are you jealous, Jupiter?" He pushed me to the edge of the pool of oil. "Do you want him?"

"Lucius —"

"You can't! He's mine!"

The Master of the World pushed me into the oil. He tore off his own purple robes of godhood. We rolled around in the slick fluid. This had to be a sacrilege! I thought. The most powerful man in the world was assaulting me, and yet I knew that to his twisted way of thinking, he was making love.

I was numb. I squeezed my eyes shut as I slipped and slid in the olive oil. I screamed in my mind — *Zeus!*

Zeus! — imagining those searching eyes, the goddess of victory in the palm of his hand, the other hand clutching a thunderbolt.

Then came thunder.

The Emperor let go of me, startled.

I climbed out of the oil. A storm had burst from a clear blue sky. The god had spoken.

Water was pouring in from the areas open to the sky, but where we stood was protected. Thunder bellowed again.

Zeus had not answered Nero; but he *had* replied to me.

All at once, our slaves were there, with strigils to wipe off the oil, fresh clothes, scents and a touch of kohl. We had never been alone. All slaves in proper Roman homes know when to be invisible, and when to materialize out of the ether. I was so glad to see Hylas that I tried to hug him; diffidently, he hung back, afraid of me. Somehow, he knew I had called the thunder.

By the time the priests and other members of our party entered the temple, there was no evidence of Nero's outburst or my humiliation. I stood beside the Emperor, trying to look as dignified as I could.

The priest returned with a retinue of lesser priests. Vespasian was there, too, with a dozen soldiers.

"We're rounding up your audience," said the general, "and we're recruiting some charioteers for the race. Strangely, no one wants to compete with you."

"Why not?" Nero said. "It's not as if I'd have them crucified if I lose."

Damnatio Memoriae · 74

XI

Chariots

There was no convenient villa for Himself to stay at, but overnight, in a nearby field, Vespasian's men had erected an entire city of tents, including a palatial one for the Divinitas.

I had never set foot in a military camp before, but this was not to be my last, as doubtless you will know from my history. But every camp I was in since then was used in actual war. This was a city manufactured in a day, with avenues, markets, even a modest arena, complete with a gold-plated statue of Himself in front of the Imperial pavilion.

Nero did not say so, but I sensed he was irked that his statue wasn't as huge as the Wonder of the World.

Tomorrow there would be the chariot race. I imagined he would cheat again by using a ten-horse chariot, not having learned from the debacle in Rome. The poetry competition would come a day later; perhaps they needed more time to round up poets.

To my surprise, the Emperor decided to sleep alone. The scene in the temple had made him irritable. He needed something — after all, he had not completed my ravishment in the pool of oil, having been interrupted by an actual god — and I was relieved that the something he needed was not going to be me. "I don't want to damage you," he said offhandedly, gorging himself on a plate of figs. I did not want to say, "The way you damaged Poppaea?" but he knew I was thinking it.

I made sure Hylas was out of sight as Himself shuffled off to a private compartment of the pavilion. There was to be a banquet that evening, but, "You take charge of it," he said.

"As Empress?" I asked him. "Or as your boy?"

"Suit yourself," he said, and vanished into his cubiculum. Two Praetorians positioned themselves in front of the entrance flap. As I turned away, a girl, gift-wrapped in silk, was being delivered to the Emperor's private quarters; I only saw strands of dark brown hair. Someone expendable.

***

Thus I came to preside over my first Imperial banquet. And because I did not have the protection of Himself, because people knew where I had come from, people did not really watch their words.

At the Imperial couch, my companion was Thaïs, the courtesan, who had travelled separately. I was glad to see her. I embraced her warmly.

"And this is the *only* place you will see me," she said, laughing, "because women aren't allowed to watch the Olympics."

"Just as well," I said, thinking of the shrieks of bloodlust one often heard from way up in the women's tier at the Circus.

At my feet sat Hylas, and Epictetus was on hand to remind me who the guests were. At the couch to my right sat the general. Beside him was the actor, Paris. Apart from some of Thaïs's protégés, there were no women, of course. The *hetairai* were sitting at the far ends of the couches, piping sweetly on double flutes, an action that Greeks find so erotic that Aristotle said that women should not be allowed to listen to this music for fear of being driven into an orgiastic frenzy.

There were plenty of guests, and the usual culinary exoticisms, such as a paté of nightingales' gizzards, but the couches next to mine were a little drama of their own. Vespasian was already a little drunk.

"What are you even doing here?" Thaïs was saying to the general. "Shouldn't you be putting down the Jewish revolt?"

"Soon enough," said Vespasian. "But why not let them have their fun a little longer? They're always going to revolt. It's in their nature. That's why this time I'm going to destroy them. I don't mean killing a few thousand of them. I mean breaking their culture, including all that is beautiful about them."

"You appreciate them," I said. "The Jews, I mean."

"What's the point of annihilating something if you don't appreciate it?" Vespasian said. And the way he looked at me said much more than quelling a rebellion in a distant province. "I'm sorry, Divinitas, I offended you in the house of the *hetaira*," he said, and gallantly knelt down to try to kiss my feet.

"No need," I said. "Will you take more wine?"

"It isn't the time," he said. "But it may yet be."

Thaïs nudged me. It was time for politics again.

"When?" I said with a smile.

"Six hundred and sixty-six," General Vespasian said softly.

"Speaking in riddles, General," I said.

"No, it's gematria," Epictetus whispered in my ear from behind the couch, "used by Jewish philosophers to code people's names into numbers, which then have magical significance. In the case of this number, it's *chi xi sigma*, which the reduction of Neron Kaisar."

"When I was in Rome," said Vespasian, "I heard this number spoken in hushed voices, in dark places."

"Someone is planning something?" Thaïs said.

"Not me," said the general. Hylas poured him more wine.

"People don't like the urine tax," Paris said. But that made the subject too obvious, so he stopped himself, and sullenly sipped more wine.

"Am I in danger?" I said.

"Personally," said Vespasian, "I *like* the urine tax. I think I'll keep it ... *Divinitas.*" Then he kissed my hand, his eyes betraying both ruthlessness and cupidity.

And thus it was I found out that my master's days were numbered. My master's and indeed my own.

And even today, I am not yet twenty.

***

The chariot races were dull. This was not the Circus Maximus. It is true that Olympia was once the world's center for chariot racing, but those days were over. The frantic crowds screaming for green, red, white and blue were absent. This audience seemed bored, if not hostile. And this was not the colossal Hippodrome that exists in Rome.

Nero, of course, appeared with his ten-horse chariot, but he need not have. His only rivals were last-minute recruits from our own legion, and they would let him win no matter what. Some of the horses were old nags. The audience had been corralled from our soldiers and had to be eked out with — such sacrilege — *women!* But since the year was not a real Olympiad year, the rules meant nothing, I suppose.

Thaïs honored the rules of society and her profession by staying away. I presided. I gave the signal. They were off.

The Divinitas won, and that was all there was to it.

***

Nero celebrated as though his victory had real meaning. The Imperial pavilion was large enough for a few dozen guests.,

Every aviary in Greece must have been plundered for the chef's most astonishing creation, an omelette made from ostrich eggs and stuffed with peacocks' brains, with a light sauce of honey, red wine, pepper, and garum, the sweet, tart, sour and salty flavors so artfully blended as to create a fifth flavor that could not be described at all.

Between courses, Himself handed out gifts: pouches crammed with aurei, jewels, title deeds to confiscated estates.

Egyptian boys wearing skimpy subligacula cavorted about, turned multiple somersaults, and constructed human pyramids. Women from Parthia wriggled about, completely covered except for their bellies, which quivered and quavered in an exotic kind of eroticism. No, this was no sober Hellenic symposium with men sitting around analyzing the Nature of the One. This was a Roman banquet — and it was fast degenerating into a Roman orgy.

But shortly after the hour of prima fax, when candles began to be lit and more lamps were brought into the pavilion, Himself abruptly took my hand and led me to his private quarters. The guests either were too drunk to notice, or too afraid to.

"Don't lie to me, Poppaea," he said.

But he was lying to himself.

"No, no, I know you're going to say you're not really Poppaea. It doesn't matter. You're the one who's here for me, here and now. I know I didn't really win," he said. "I *do* know that, Sporus."

"It doesn't matter," I said.

"Why did I try to argue with Zeus?" he said. "He sent that thunderbolt. Everyone saw it. Is my hubris to be my downfall? I have no thunder. No volcanoes, no tempests. I don't control the winds, the floods. Only people."

"People love you," I said.

"Don't lie to me. I killed my mother. I killed my wife. I'll kill you, too. Just wait."

"Yes, Lucius," I said softly. "Whenever you like."

At that moment, I did not know whether I would survive the night.

"The poetry contest," Nero said. "That's *real*. That's about truth, and beauty. If it is hubris that afflicts me, I'll transform it into a true paean to the human condition. They'll all be in tears. I'll win that one. As *myself*."

"You deserve to be happy," I said.

"Then make me happy," he said. He embraced me with real tenderness. He was weeping. I dried his cheeks with my lips.

His grief, it seemed, was unquenchable. I did not really know how I could be of any help. But what I knew how to do, I did. And shortly after, he descended into fitful slumber.

XIII

SACRIFICES

In succeeding days, the Emperor brooded, demanded to be left alone with his lyre, or rehearsed by himself, sometimes using Lucius Domitius Paris as a sounding-board.

I wandered with Hylas through the fields and avenues of Olympia, managing to avoid being recognized much of the time by the simple expedient of not dressing as a member of the Imperial family.

Freed from having to entertain the Master of the World, we were able to wander down byways, stopping to buy souvenirs, and to pray at the temple of Zeus, which was by no means as intimidating as when I had been there with the Emperor.

Everywhere they were selling bowls, *kylixes*, and vases with the inscription *ho pais kalós* and images of beautiful boys, for here people like me and Hylas were celebrated in a way that decent Romans would've probably found a little embarrassing. There were so many athletes, many wandering in casual nudity, that Hylas and I did not really attract any attention. While there were stares from time to time, there were few lewd comments or whistles.

At night, the Emperor was too worn out to make demands on his beleaguered Empress. It could almost be said that those days of preparation were idyllic.

Inevitably, however, would come disappointment.

After days of feeling quite liberated came the day of the poetry competition. The Emperor rose long before dawn and took me by the hand. We walked along almost deserted avenues: past the temples, past the Palestra, past the stadium, past rows of statues of victors of contests, sometimes sculpted centuries ago, but still lovingly painted to seem still real, still beautiful, still in the bloom of youth. Past olive groves, past souvenir stands, where even now they were setting up their wares.

This was the same avenue I had walked down hand in hand with Hylas. The same market, the same temples, the same groves ... but these things were not the same.

For I knew that just out of sight, there lurked a detachment of Praetorians ready to protect the emperor at a moment's notice.

We did have the illusion of being alone. But I was acutely aware that it was an illusion. Himself, perhaps not as aware.

Himself took me to a grove far from the temporary tent city the army had built. We stood in a circle of olive trees. An old marble herm with archaic, angular features looked down on us. There was a little altar to Apollo. Piled around it were old lyres, many of them weathered and worn. This was the place where great artists dedicated their music to the god.

Nero took me in his arms and kissed me chastely on the cheek. Fearful, I felt myself going limp. But he was showing me a kind of tenderness.

He said, "I haven't really had time for you, dearest. But a few hours from now I'm going to have my great moment, before all the gods. So I wanted to do something just for you."

"I am happy, Lucius," I said.

"Well, I want to make a sacrifice. And sing you a song. A song I made just for you."

He snapped his fingers. Out of nowhere, a slave appeared and handed him a small, sealed jar. It was old, painted with classic, black-figure images; one side represented a boy with an eagle, Ganymede I imagined. The other was a goddess, Aphrodite perhaps, for she seemed to be stepping out of the sea.

"You can't fool me," Nero said. "I was never fooled. I've always known who you really are."

"But …" I said. "You don't say anything, because it would break the spell." I hoped I sounded thoughtful and not full of panic, as I desperately sought to find a way to cling to whatever shred of identity was left to me.

"Let's offer it together," said Himself.

He placed my hand on the jar along with his. Something in the jar was sloshing, and I wondered whether this was a fine wine we were offering up.

"Aren't you glad I saved them?" the Emperor said.

I felt hollow. I felt empty. I had to contrive a witty, worldly response. "Well, at least I will be whole in the next world," I said. It was all I could do to keep from vomiting.

"I know," he said. "I'll want you complete when we are in Olympus." I think he was trying to apologize.

As we held the jar up, he held me closer to him. He took my severed organs and laid them on the altar, among the ancient lyres. "Apollo," he whispered, "as you loved Hyancinthos, I love Sporus."

He kissed me again. There was no passion, but there was a strange sincerity.

When he released me, he said, "You see, I do know your real name."

He did not; my real name died with Hyacinth, because he alone spoke the language that my true name could be spoken in.

But I did not tell him that. "Yes, Divinitas," was all I said.

Himself lit the flame at the altar — rather it was lit for him by a slave who somehow managed to be invisible — and put in a pinch of incense. Or rather, a pinch of incense was discreetly dropped in by another slave. Sweet smoke welled up, making it easier for the slaves to disappear; it was like a conjurer's trick. Nero turned to me.

"Now that we've made the sacrifice together," he said, "you probably know I have been thinking a lot about what lies on the other side."

"The other side?"

"Of the river."

By which, of course, he meant death. The only being who regularly makes the crossing of the Styx, then returns to the world above, is Persephone. And that is the role it seems I am fated to play, in the end.

"I know I won't be here much longer," he said. "That's why I brought you to Greece. To know where we are going, we must first comprehend where we come from. We must come to the source of our being to understand ourselves."

"What makes you think it's coming to an end?" I asked him.

"I hear things. There are plots."

"But you've always managed to suppress plots," I said, thinking of the dozens, perhaps hundreds, of suspected traitors who had been executed or ordered to commit suicide. Including all the innocent ones. Like my patronus.

"Every escape is narrower than the last."

"But you have the Praetorians."

"Who can be bought. No, no, my dear, there is almost no one who doesn't feel a bit of rancor or resentment. For a god, I am quite put upon."

"Actë," I said.

"Yes, Actë. And you."

It was true enough. For all that he had violated me in the most hateful of ways, I had never wished him ill.

"That's why you must make me a promise. I mean, I've undone the wrong I did you ... or at least, I will have undone it in the next life. Now, I want you to swear that you will be with me when that moment comes. It will be bloody, I know. And you're one of the few who understands ... how lonely it is to be a god."

"And a man."

"Yes. Like the god of those Chrestianoi. Maybe I should have thrown *my* worshippers to the lions. In a world without sycophants, I'd have a clearer view."

"You're not alone," I said.

"*You'd* never lie to me," he said.

"No," I lied.

A lyre appeared in his hands. He motioned for me to sit, and I did so on a stone bench in front of the herm. And then he sang.

Not in the Greek of immortal poets, but in plain Latin, the language of the mob, the language you speak when you're among close friends, the language you speak to slaves.

> *I strive with the winds*
> *but soon I will go*
> *where everyone else has gone*
> *wisdom and beauty are never found together*
> *but in you, youth, they are;*
> *seek other shores; seek adventures;*
> *but as for me, love pinches*
> *like an old crab*

There were no fanciful apostrophes to mythical beings. No protests against the Fates. No plaints to the Nine Muses. And to go with the words, Nero had found a melody that was almost like a folksong. Since moving to the palace I had walled off my heart and mind, but I felt my reserve crumbling. Hadn't I once fallen stupidly in love with him, when he was distant and impossible to get close to, when I was nobody? Then again, how long had those feelings lasted?

Tears were welling up when it slowly dawned on me that Nero had stolen these words. No wonder they sounded familiar. They were lines lifted wholesale from Petronius's *Satyricon,* scrambled and served up together like a dish of eggs and honey.

The Master of the World was a thief. He stole words. He stole Divinity itself. He had stolen my dreams. And, as he looked deeply into my eyes, *I knew that he knew this.*

Now I was really weeping. I was mourning my patronus as I never had before. I poured out all my pent-up sorrow.

Nero knew I did not weep for him.

He did know me, you see.

There was a boy named Lucius Domitius who had been banished from court together with his ambitious, stiflingly protective mother. He had grown up among slaves. He had spoken Latin all day long, like ordinary people. He had loved Actë. He had known, as humans understand the word, happiness.

One day, he had been summoned back to Rome, and Rome had devoured him and left him without a heart.

Lucius Domitius had become Nero Claudius Caesar Augustus Germanicus, Pater Patriae, Pontifex Maximus, the Living God.

Lucius Domitius was dead.

Yet, long after Nero had buried him, it was Lucius Domitius who truly saw me.

XIV

Songs without Words

The poetry competition seemed to take place in a completely different world, for even though chariot racing was born in Olympia, its frenzied, bloodlust-driven apotheosis was in the Circus Maximus. Yet the crowning glory of Olympia was as the birthplace of poesy.

There was a litter waiting by the side of Apollo's Grove. It must have been there all along, but somehow it conveniently hove into view just at the moment when we needed to be transported somewhere.

It was a covered litter and inside, it was capacious enough for two slaves kneeling at the ready to be able to apply fresh cosmetics to the Emperor and to change his simple garments to the resplendent attire of a master poet.

The metamorphosis took but a few minutes and I watched with amazement at the slaves fussed over my master, working with both skill and celerity.

By the time we arrived at the theater where the competition was to take place, the Master of the World was also its mistress. For he had decided to perform his showpiece, the "Grief of Niobe." They had erected a pavilion for him to prepare in, but he wanted to watch his rivals. At the same time, he did not want to reveal his costume. "Just throw a big cloak and a veil over me," he said. "No one will know it's me."

Everyone *did* know, of course. But no one said anything.

It was an ancient amphitheater of the kind so cunningly built that it could reflect the briefest whisper and make the entire place reverberate. It could take a whimper of pain, a moan of pleasure, and turn them into world-shattering outbursts of emotion.

When we arrived at our seats, it was already midmorning. An old man was performing. His narration was a classic subject: King Priam, begging vengeful Achilles for the body of his son Hector. But the poet, instead of using an epic meter and epic language, had recast the monologue into a lyric form and used the Aeolic dialect as though this were something written by Sappho. In the background, a chorus of boys dressed as Trojan women were sighing and swaying back and forth in a strange parody of grief. It was all very modern, and you could tell that the audience wasn't having it. In these competitions, the audience is very knowledgeable and nothing much gets by them.

When the old man had finished, there was desultory applause and a few cheers from a small claque, who were obviously his very special devotees. He bowed a few times and exited with his entire chorus, who gyrated in a rather unorthodox choreography as they followed him off stage.

"What passes for art these days," Nero murmured from beneath his veil.

Next came three more Niobes that had been scheduled in today's program. Each was more hysterical than the last; it had been unwise of the organizers to put all three of them one after the other. I remembered that my own Lord and Master considered himself an expert at this role. It's very easy to move an audience with a speech in which you are surrounded by dozens of your dead and dying children. And Nero's version of Niobe was considered particularly gut-wrenching, not to mention overlong. By the time the Niobes were done, it was well past mid-afternoon.

At any other athletic or artistic event, there would be vendors selling exotic delicacies, and our audience would have been munching on sausages or cakes or quaffing wine. But, as I say, they take their poetry very seriously in Olympia, and the crowd listened with rapt attention, even to the third Niobe, who was extremely wearying to listen to. It was not a good day for the vendors.

An announcer declared that there was now going to be a special unannounced competitor. I looked up. I admit I had been nodding off. At this moment, too, several members of the Emperor's entourage appeared and took their seats behind me. Among them was the general, Titus Flavius Vespasianus. There were also members of my household staff and that of the Emperor's. They had been waiting until now because they did not want to sit through a lot of men portraying hysterical women in maudlin verse.

During this entire time Himself, the Divine Nero, had been sitting next to me in the Imperial box, which was not a separate structure as it would have been in Rome, but simply a partitioned section of the best seats. Himself had been watching the competitors intently and as it became clear to him that none of them was his equal, he had allowed himself a little smile, especially when the third of the three Niobes was shrieking.

He turned to me and he said, "I'm far more of a woman than they'll ever be". And he poked me in the rib, thinking this a very fine joke and seeming to have forgotten the womanhood he himself had inflicted upon me without asking.

I suppose we were anxious to see who the surprise competitor would be, but no one was as surprised as Himself. For the man who walked over to the center of the scenic was no less a figure than Lucius Domitius Paris himself. And Paris, too, was Niobe. *Another* Niobe. This Niobe was wearing a simple cloak, as though awakened from sleep to the horror that had been wreaked on her children.

The Emperor sputtered, "How could he, how dare he!"

There was no chorus. There was no ensemble of *kitharas* and flutes. Only a single four-stringed lyre. Paris waved for the music to begin. We were all waiting for the sound of his voice, celebrated by critics and music lovers throughout the empire. But he did not sing. The lyre sounded ... just one note, again and again.

Nero whispered, "I brought him here to help train me, not to undermine me!"

Then Paris spoke. Again, he did not sing. After a brief introductory strophe and antistrophe, Paris stopped his recitation, and allowed the lyre-players to play, just a repetitive sequence of notes, a slow ostinato that seemed meaningless enough but grew in force and obsessive power until the sound produced was overwhelming.

And Paris *mimed* the tale of Niobe's grief. This was his surprise! He had not entered the *singing* competition at all — he was not going to sing a note. *This* was his revenge against the poetaster Emperor's mediocrity.

Paris was alone on stage but as he played all the roles — the gods, the tormented princess, the innocent boys and girls — you could see all fourteen children riddled with arrows as the twin gods, sun and moon, hunted them down and shot them. You could hear their screams, the shock of the palace servants, the swoosh of celestial darts as they found their marks, the rending of flesh, the spurt of blood and the gush of tears. All without Paris making a single sound.

I looked around. People were in tears.

Nero muttered, "I begged him to teach me mime. *Begged* him! He refused. He refused *me!* And I now I know — he always intended to make a fool of me!"

Nero rose from his seat and began to storm away. I got up to follow, but he sternly waved at me to sit back down. "You must represent Rome," he said. He left, and a dozen Praetorians went with him.

Paris had still not sung. What I witnessed next was extraordinary. I saw the spirit of Niobe slowly dissolve, like wine poured into sand, and the actor emerge. It happened slowly. It was as if Niobe had possessed his body and soul, and now was gradually dissociating herself from him. And what remained was an actor, an empty vessel.

There was a stunned silence.

The applause came like a storm at sea.

Lucius Domitius Paris, I thought, *is a dead man.*

XV

Madness

We waited. I do not know how long, but it was far longer than the time it should take to set up the next contestant. In fact, the sun was beginning to set. I realize now that the Divine Nero was planning to use the sunset as part of his performance, as though, like the gods themselves, he could control the very movements of the celestial bodies.

First, there came a deafening fanfare from a dozen cornua and bucinae along with the pounding of sets of tympana and the wail of a water organ. The musicians were concealed behind the *skene*, so it seemed that the music was rising from the walls and the mountains.

Then entered a chorus of fourteen boys, seven of them garbed as girls, in a fantastical imagined recreation of archaic Mycenaean court dress. They wore masks as in an ancient play by Euripides. They sang an ode to the beauty of their mother, Niobe, and of her pride in her many children, which had challenged the fecundity of the mighty goddess Leto, parent of Apollo and Artemis.

The lilting melody was interrupted when the overhead machina was activated and Artemis and Apollo descended from the sky. They were carrying golden bows and immediately began shooting arrows from overhead. The audience gasped. A child clutched his stomach as blood spurted.

I heard people behind me: "This is *real!*"

Surely, this couldn't really be happening. But the gods did not stop shooting arrows until every child lay in a pool of blood. Then they entered the machina and were carried back up to Olympus. This was carrying realism too far. Surely, the theater was not the Circus. Surely, these were not some hapless criminals condemned to die for our entertainment. They were chorus boys with beautiful high voices.

Then, as the children lay there, as the crowd whispered and murmured, as I watched in consternation, another god entered, this time from somewhere beneath the stage. Dark was his aspect and he wore a dark cloak and held in his hand a pomegranate. I knew that this had to be Hades, god of death.

Hades walked among the dead children. He touched each one gently with his pomegranate. As he did so, a flute played, a melody of aching loveliness, a melody that sobbed and soared. A miracle was occurring. Each child was coming back to life. It had been theater after all, and not some execution of cheap slaves. Stagehands, dressed in black tunics, emerged with mops to remove all traces of the stage blood.

Then the applause began. It was not forced applause. The audience had had a true catharsis, believing Niobe's children had really died, then feeling true joy and relief when the god revived them.

The chorus stood and bowed to the audience. Then Hades dismissed them, and they left the *proskenion*, each boy holding hands with a boy-girl.

I really wished I could be there with them. They died and they got back up again. This evening, they would go home to their families or their lovers. Acting ended with the end of the play.

But my life was not like theirs. I was never allowed to stop acting. I even had to act after I lost consciousness each night, making sure I fell asleep in an elegant position, tucking myself into my Emperor's arms in case he wanted me without awakening me. The hours of freedom — wandering the market with Hylas, for instance — were rare, and would probably end completely once we returned to Rome.

There came another deafening fanfare, and Hades slowly walked to the front of the stage. A cloud of smoke appeared from nowhere, enveloping him completely as the music welled up and then died away. Smoke filled the amphitheater. Some started to cough. Others, I think, were afraid something was on fire.

The fog cleared. The god of death stood there no longer.

Instead, it was the Living God. It was my husband. It was Nero Claudius Caesar Augustus Germanicus, Master of the World and would-be laureate of the greatest crown in poetry. And only then did Nero launch into his song, his own version of the grief of Niobe.

This was a version I had heard before. It was by no means dull. Nero modulated his voice, producing an enormous range of emotion from grief to madness to bittersweet remembrances of Niobe's children. Nero had skill, and he had practiced every melisma to perfection.

I knew this was Nero's finest public performance. And yet I was unmoved.

I remember, though, that while the public had been entertained by the gimmickry of the opening, Nero's singing impressed them on a higher level. Nero loved this music and he made it his. He really did have talent. If only he had not been Emperor ... what an artist he could have been! And perhaps he would not have been driven mad.

For this was the same voice that had once convinced me that Nero's art had deep and thoughtful sources. The Emperor had thought out every inflection, every vocal ornament. Yet, there was something that I had never noticed before. There was an emptiness.

Perhaps it was because when he had sung to me earlier that morning I had realized that he had merely regurgitated the words of my beloved patronus. I no longer felt sincerity. I remembered his true self, I remembered how he had sung to me, alone, in the grove of Apollo.

This was not the real Nero. This, like me in my role as the Empress-Eromenos of the Divinitas, was acting. It was not entirely sincere, yet I believed that Himself believed it to be. Truth and lies had become so interwoven in his mind that there was no distinction between them.

But looking around me, I could see that the audience, this most sophisticated and knowledgeable of all audiences, was not unmoved. Indeed, the performance was well worthy of receiving a laurel wreath.

The entire display of color, spectacle, and drama at the beginning had not really been necessary. Nero could have just walked onto the stage and begun. It was perhaps insecurity that had made him adorn his performance with such extravagances.

In a while, the Divinity settled into a long catalog of miseries. Niobe recounted every slight, every painful exchange between her and the goddess Leto, who envied her fourteen children yet became enraged by her hubris.

It was during this rather long-winded segment of Nero's narration that I became aware that someone behind me was snoring. I tried to ignore it, but the snores became quite intrusive. I did not want to turn around for fear that Nero might notice that I was not giving him my full attention. But as the singing continued, the snoring crescendoed, and since it too was accentuated by the echoing acoustic of this amphitheater, I knew that the snores would eventually be heard by Himself.

Slowly I turned to see if I could detect the source. Snoring at a poetry reading is already reprehensible, but when a god himself declaims, surely it might even merit the death penalty. So I sneaked a look behind me. The snorer was none other than the great general himself, Vespasian.

The snoring became so loud that it was competing with Himself, interjecting a percussive accompaniment to his singing.

Then the unthinkable happened.

Nero was singing the words *pheu, pheu* on a series of high falsetto long notes. The highest, purest, most beautiful of the notes was rudely truncated by a particularly loud snore.

The Emperor stopped in mid-note.

He glared at the audience, and his eye alighted on the snoring general.

Nero exploded. He flung his lyre at the spectators. He missed the general completely and struck an old man in the chest. The man slumped forward. The audience rose to its feet. The Emperor stalked off the *proskenion* and vanished into the building behind the stage.

The second he was gone, they were speaking all at once. Their rapt attention had been shattered in an instant. I heard some whisper *sacrilege*. Olympia could not be profaned — Olympia, the heart of the Hellenic identity, the icon of cultural leadership in a conquered land.

As the hubbub continued, General Vespasian finally woke up.

"What happened?" he said, rubbing his eyes.

One of his Praetorians said, "You've insulted the Emperor." Other soldiers were laughing.

The general rose from his seat. He turned to me, and I got up too.

"It seems that I must go, my pretty one," he said.

"Where?"

"I'm needed in Judaea. There's a revolt than needs suppressing."

"But the Emperor's wrath —"

"Your beloved is not long for this world. And you must know who actually rules in Rome. The army. Your God is just a propped-up puppet, Sporus. The tide has turned."

"The tide? But who will protect me?"

"It's every man for himself. Or herself. As for me, my only option is clear: huge military success in far-off Judaea, something really epic. Perhaps I'll burn down their temple, capture whatever is inside their Holy of Holies, enslave everyone in Jerusalem — oh, there'll be a market glut of pretty, dark-haired boys without foreskins, but you'll still be the only blonde without balls! I'll be ruthless. And when I have been ruthless enough that all the world fears me, I will march back to RomeItaly and mop up any mess that has been left in your pathetic Emperor's wake. And if you survive the chaos"— mockingly, he kissed my hand — "perhaps a wedding to the former Empress Poppaea could lend my reign legitimacy."

And with that, he gestured to his men. Smartly, as one, they turned and tramped out of the theater.

Only two Praetorians remained.

XVI

Ubi Gaius Ego Gaia

Despite the outburst, or more likely because of it, the laurels were awarded to the Divinitas. He did not even have to complete his performance.

Since his amazing performance entirely in mime, Paris had not reappeared. Perhaps he was already on his homeward journey. Indeed, I imagined him riding alongside General Vespasian, perhaps bound for Judea, so that they could both escape the long arm of the Emperor's wrath.

The award ceremony was not attended by any of the contestants. Perhaps they had all already gone home. The judges consisted of a panel of elders who spoke briefly in turn before proffering the laurels to the Divinity. He did not humble himself to receive them but took them from the hands of the chief judge and placed them on his own head. Surely in his heart he must have known that Paris had outclassed him utterly without even singing a single note of music.

The ceremony did not take long. The judges said their congratulatory remarks, but they were all platitudes.

A handful of soldiers remained to escort Himself to the encampment. The Emperor and I sat on an open litter this time, presumably so he could show off his laurels and be admired by the crowd of admirers, only there was not much of a crowd.

There were a few curious onlookers, though. As we passed them, they bowed low. Some even fell on their knees. There was a sense of unease, an atmosphere of dread. After people paid their respects, they slunk sullenly away.

Presently, there was almost no one left lining the avenue except for some bored-looking children. And then there were none of those, even.

To reach the tent city, the party had to make a sharp turn and pass through some woods. They then descended a gentle incline to reach the shallow valley where the Emperor's headquarters had been built in only a day.

It was when we emerged from the forest that we could see a crowd congregating. They were all standing around a wooden post from which something was dangling. It looked a bit like a human being, but it could not have been one. We came closer. The crowd saw us and immediately backed away. They looked at us in horror.

The Emperor ordered his litter to stop and, taking me by the hand, led me to take a closer look. People scrambled out of the way. I couldn't help letting out a little scream when I saw what it was.

Nailed to the wooden post was an almost intact, flayed human skin, the arms and legs folded like cloth. The head, what was left of it — the face that is — was warped and folded beyond recognition. But I knew who it was.

"I couldn't very well have him crucified," Himself said, shaking his head. "He's a Roman citizen."

"Does it satisfy you?" I said.

"No," he said.

"What will?"

The Emperor said, "He wouldn't teach me the art of mime. And now he never will. His art has died as well."

"This," I sighed, "is what happens when you challenge the gods." For I knew that the Emperor was recreating the story of Marsyas, who had dared to claim to play the flute more beautifully than Apollo. They had engaged in a competition, with the winner being allowed to do anything he wanted to the loser. Apollo elected to have Marsyas flayed alive and hung his skin upon a pine tree. That is how the story goes.

"Thus," said Nero, "we see the consequences of hubris."

I said, "Lucius, surely this was too high a price to pay."

Nero replied, "To challenge the gods is a blasphemy for which there is no such thing as too high a price to pay!" And then he began to quote the words of the poet Ovid.

> *"quid me mihi detrahis?" inquit;*
> *"a! piget, a! non est" clamabat "tibia tanti."*

I repeated the words, translating them into Greek: "Why are you tearing me apart? A flute is not worth a life!"

Ovid's lines spoke of dismemberment and music but somehow the incessant rhythm of the hexameters made something beautiful out of what should have been gruesome and distasteful.

"But he would not teach me mime," said the Master of the World. "He could have just taught me. He kept something in reserve, something which he knew could be used to defeat me."

I said, "You're not defeated, Lucius. You're alive, and he's not."

He turned to the flayed skin, which was flapping about now as a wind rose, pulling against the nails. "Do you hear that?" He shook his fist as he addressed the remains of Lucius Domitius Paris. "I'm alive and you're not!" Shouting to his attendants, cowering in the background, he said, "Bring me my lyre!"

"It's broken, Lucius," I said.

Hylas was the only one bold enough to bring it to him. The frame was dented, and two of the four strings had snapped. Oblivious, Nero seized it and began strumming on the two remaining strings, which had loosened and now twanged and thwacked against the soundboard.

He sang, his voice breaking, pausing between words to curse or to weep:

O son of Leto...

and I realized that he was finishing the performance at the contest that had been interrupted by his fury, continuing with an apostrophe to Apollo.

He rasped out the final strophes of the soliloquy, his voice a grotesque parody of the hysterical Niobe.

The song ended. No one came to gawk. He had driven away the crowd, this man who thrived on having an audience.

"What about it, Vespasian?" he shouted. "Are you still snoring?"

"Lucius," I said softly, "he's gone to Judaea."

"I gave him no such permission."

"You commanded it," I said. "He is to burn down their temple, enslave the entire city of Jerusalem, and bring back whatever's inside their sanctum sanctorum to lay at your feet."

"I commanded *that?*"

Taking a lead from Petronius's art of manipulating the Emperor, I said, "Only you could have conceived of a spectacle so epic, so magnificent, so *total*."

"Oh," he said. "I had forgotten."

"Yes, Divinitas," I said.

"*I had forgotten!*" I knew that he meant he thought I was lying. He turned to Paris's flayed skin again. "I don't remember ordering *you* killed, either," he said, though now I knew *he* was lying. "I forgive you," he said. "You can come back to life now. You can return. Just as Hades sent Persephone back to the land of the living, I order you back."

It sounded like one of the things the god of the Chrestianoi was rumored to be able to do. *Where is the line between the real world and the world of the insane?* I wondered. And at what point had Himself crossed over to where there was no longer any turning back?

I could sense a tantrum coming on. Nero believed there were no limits to his power, but General Vespasian had told me quite clearly that the limits were there. The limits did not depend on extravagance or cruelty. It was the army that tolerated the foibles ... and the army who would replace the Emperor ... in its own time.

The few soldiers who remained were no doubt ordered to obey the Emperor without question until such time as they received other orders. So at this moment, all our lives were in danger. Nero was furious, and did not know *why* he was furious. Only I knew that his rage was ultimately directed inward, at himself, and that Himself was the one person he dared not punish.

I had to break the spell.

"Lucius," I said, "let's get married."

"What do you mean? We *are* married."

"No, *you* married *me* while I was unconscious from pain and poppy juice. I did not even know it had happened."

"You mean a proper Roman ceremony, with a priest and witnesses?" I could sense his mania halting and turning a corner.

"Yes!" I said. "And a proper Roman banquet."

"Oh yes," he said, kissing me passionately as Lucius Domitius Paris's flayed skin flapped in the breeze of sunset. It was a kiss of tenderness as well as terror, of purity as well as insecurity. I felt them all, all those emotions; I was the mirror of all these feelings, unchecked and unrestrained; I had to receive the entirety of the tempest all alone; all this, and I was a boy of not even twenty.

When he broke away at last, I turned to see my people, Croesus and Hylas, and the Emperor's staff, Epictetus and others, drawing close. I said to them, to no one in particular, "A wedding. A priest. Guests. Nobility. Entertainment. A banquet."

And by magic, all those things were produced out of thin air.

And thus it was that I, in full bridal costume, stood hand in hand with the Living God, and spoke the words, "Where thou art Gaius, I am Gaia."

In the night, he reached for me, sobbing.

"Our beautiful dream is over," he said.

In that moment, I did love him.

XVII

Foreshadowings

So you have a plan. If you hold out long enough, Titus Flavius Vespasianus will ride to the rescue at the head of a huge army, and you'll be saved.

I doubt he'd bother to save me.

Why not? You told me he flirted with you.

Vespasian has something the last four Emperors lacked: sense.

Is it sensible to destroy an entire province and enslave its entire population?

Not from the point of view of the Judaeans. But see this as a future Emperor might. Why not sacrifice the Jews on the altar of stability? Think of the triumphal arches, the commemorative coinage with the words *Judaea Capta* imprinted for the entire world to see, think of how this would

show the Empire that Rome cannot be withstood by anyone ... let alone by the one god of a distant desert tribe.

I cannot imagine that he will come for me.

Thanks to you, I've already met my death. My big, beautiful, dark demise. I am sure the pain will be both exquisite and excruciating. But I've accepted it. If I could be a real god in life, why not a false god in death? Petronius would have loved such an irony.

***

We are on the ship now. There was no triumphal progress. We took to sea as soon as we could, with only the minimum of pomp. On the way to Greece, I had been drugged and mostly in a stupor. On the way home, the voyage seemed endless. I had plenty of time to reflect about myself, about who I was, and what I would have to do if the unthinkable happened.

And so it was that one night, under the stars, in the midst of the sea, I stood with my slave Hylas, with Croesus not far off, and told him I was going to set him free.

"I don't want that," he said, his Latin now almost. "You know I don't."

"But you are my slave," I said, "so it must be what *I* want."

"Don't you love me anymore?" Hylas said.

I beckoned Croesus to come to us with the documents of manumission.

"I can't truly love you," I said, "if you are not my equal."

He looked at me for a long time. Then he said, "You think you're going to die."

***

He was right, and the time for that draws ever closer.

But before it happens, there's more to tell you.

Nero's decline was precipitous and all the Emperors that followed in swift succession were each of them very different. And all of them, save one, loved me.

Let me rest now, and we will go on in the morning.

XVIII

The Sea

Joyful or mournful?
The same gulls, crying over the same sea.
The Romans call it *Mare Nostrum* ... *our* sea.
Arrogance, or acknowledgment?
Tell me, Sporus.
***

My life, short though it will have been, falls, like a chorus of Euripides or an ode by Pindar, into clear, contrasting segments, each delineated by water. Like classic Greek poetry: first a strophe, then an antistrophe, matching each other perfectly in scansion yet often saying each other's opposite. And an epode at the end that brings the opposites into harmony, constrained by the art and artifice of the poet's command of the language ...

It sounds pretentious, Empress. Days have gone by, and still we're waiting for you to go onstage and make your grand exit from the world. I don't know why it hasn't happened yet. I can understand your wanting to find some kind of order to your chaotic life. But your life ... a Greek ode?

Hear me out. I've had some time to think about it. You've made me up and cleaned me up and made me up again so many times, preparing me for the brutal execution that keeps getting put off. I wouldn't recognize my real face anymore, not in the finest polished mirror.

A Greek ode?

First, the idyllic childhood that I barely remember, followed by my capture and being sent in chains by sea to Rome. Then, my life with my beloved patronus, the intrigue at court, the path that led me from slave boy to a fateful meeting with the Lord of the World. And after being viciously mutilated, stripped of my maleness, another journey by sea to the heart of civilization, where I learned just how precarious this monumental edifice called Rome really is, and where I finally came to understand that this world I know can disintegrate on a whim.

Between each stanza of my life, there is the sea.

There was the sea that brought me to Rome. Every gust of wind, every unfamiliar scent, every cry of a distant seagull was terrifying to me. I felt the sea through a miasma of pain.

My second journey, the antistrophe to this ode: knowing all I knew, great poetry and art and music crammed into my mind by the greatest minds of Rome, a trek to the very heart of civilization ... all the hope in the world ... all the joy, yet tempered by the fact that I had lost something I could never get back....

And now, it was my third voyage.

I had arrived with despair and discovered, in the darkness, hidden reserves of hope.

I had left again with new hopes, only to find them dashed by the corruption in Olympia, the world's icon of fairness and of unpolluted devotion to beauty and goodness.

And now I was returning, knowing in my heart that we were doomed: I, of course, because my very identity had never been my own, those close to me, because their fate was tied to mine, and mine in turn to the fate of Himself the God, the Divine Emperor, Lord of the World, Nero Claudius Caesar Augustus Germanicus, Father of the Country, Pontifex Maximus, whose name, because of an edict of Damnatio Memoriae, may no longer be spoken.

You haven't even told me your name.

Do I need one? I am just a slave, working for the editor of these grand games of triumph. I am treated well, because my skills are rare and valuable, but if your death doesn't rise to the appropriate level of epic drama, I'll probably get a beating.

Before you send me out to the arena to be raped to death by a monster dressed as Hades, whisper your name to me.

So I can be the last person you think about?

Anyone but Nero.

XIX

TRIUMPH

And so, after Nero's so-called victories in the Olympics, you and your Divine Companion returned to the Eternal City in triumph.

Oh yes. A triumph! Parades! Honours! A temporary increase in the bread dole! Free baths for a month! Lottery tickets with country estates and all-night tokens for the city's priciest, naughtiest lupanar!

And of course, games!

Like these games?

Games like these — the ones I'm going to be killed in — well, a little more spectacular, nothing so measly as today's sorry spectacle. There's not enough gold left in the whole world for the kind of extravaganza we witnessed in the last days of Nero Claudius Caesar Augustus Germanicus, my Husband and God.

I've heard that certain legendary animals are now extinct because of those games. Sea-unicorns — dragons — camelopards — wyverns —

Dragons! I see those games have become even more legendary in the memory!

I didn't believe it either.

Games, yes — bigger and more splendid and more innovative than ever before. The Divinity had not merely triumphed over barbarians — he had conquered the very heart of civilization. He did not just own the bodies of his subjects — he possessed their souls — he had remade art and music in the image of Himself.

But first there was the triumphal procession itself. Nero dispensed with the traditional whisperer in the chariot who was supposed to say, constantly, "Remember, thou art mortal." He was, after all, a god.

He had ten white horses dyed green so no one could mistake whose colors he favored. I was in the procession, too, as Venus, stepping from a giant golden scallop shell, with nymphs around me to hold up feathered fans to hide those parts the crowd might have been curious about. I was the perfect object of love, both boy and girl, both child and immortal.

Though Vespasian's legions had sailed to Judaea, there was of course the Praetorian Guard, still under the command of the sadistic Tigellinus and the seedy Nymphidius, who had stopped trying to molest me in the hidden corners of the palace since I had become the new Poppaea. Though he continued to molest me with his eyes.

There were plenty of Praetorians marching in the triumph. As the Divinitas had told me when we arrived,

"They at least will be loyal to the last, since they're paid three and a half times as much as ordinary legionaries. *And* they're getting a special donativum in honour of our wedding."

Yes. Our military might must be bought and paid for, or it all falls apart. As Vespasian told me ... it is the one sure truth that underpins our Roman way of life.

***

It was dawn and we had only been back from Greece for a day or two. His Majesty himself had arrived just as unannounced as he had departed, and it would take some time to pull together all the spectacles that he needed to be devised for his triumphal return. But meanwhile, given that General Vespasian had a very large army, even though it was moving further and further to the east ... the Praetorians needed to be massaged a bit.

"It's about money again, isn't it?" I said, as we lay once more in the cubiculum where I had seen Poppaea kicked to death.

This room, heavily perfumed to cover the omnipresent traces of an aroma of spilt wine with hints of vomit and of cheetah piss, with Hercules on his golden leash at the foot of the bed, and my body-slave Hylas hiding behind the drapes, now felt like home. That was the oddest thing of all, how this most unreal of environments had come to have a sense of familiarity, of welcome even. I lay back, allowing Himself to explore my body with his hands, to peer at my pores through eyepieces of polished ruby, sapphire and emerald.

"It seems to be healing well," he said, running his finger over the scar. It no longer pained me. But the

Divinitas's touch did not bring the kind of automatic arousal that might have happened in the past. It was just a touch. "You're not feeling any pleasure," he said.

"A kind of pleasure, perhaps," I said. But I was surprised he even asked; he rarely thought of anyone's pleasure but his own. "Thank you for asking," I said, and kissed Himself lightly on the cheek.

Suddenly he turned from me, sat up. "The army," he said. "The cursed *army!*"

"It *is* about money, then," I said. "It's time to pay them off."

"And every time I do it, I give them more, and it buys me a shorter span of protection."

"How much do we need?"

"Don't worry your pretty little head about such sordid details, my love," said the Divinitas. "However much it is, it won't be worth as much as a single hair from your precious, delicate pubis." He proceeded to pluck one. Such was his idea of an erotic conversation.

"Don't," I said. "I've few enough of those as it is." Indeed, since my mutilation, no new ones. "Though if they are worth that much, surely you can pay off the Praetorians with one."

He laughed, and then became suddenly very thoughtful.

"You actually mean to do it!"

"Don't be silly," the Emperor said. "And yet ... I have the most brilliant idea, Sporus. *You* will be the one to present the donativum. That way, they will all see and acknowledge their Empress, and it will dispel the misguided rumour that somehow Poppaea was mysteriously murdered by someone or other!" I wanted to roll my eyes, but he seemed much taken by this new conceit. So I just looked at him with that look of girlish adoration that he loved to see in me.

***

I prepared myself for another stupefyingly dull ceremony, in which I would have to sit stiffly enthroned and be charming and Empress-like, while slaves handed out pouches full of money to all six thousand or so members of the Praetorian Guard.

This was not what transpired, however. It was a private event, and only a few dozen of the most important Praetorians were there. It was more in the manner of a morning salutatio, the kind my patronus, Petronius, had every morning, no matter how enervating the previous night's orgy had been. Of course, being the Emperor's salutatio, there was more ritual and more grovelling, and more at stake — life and death, even.

It had taken me a very long morning to be made up and sumptuously dressed as the Empress. It had taken almost longer to get to the Emperor's new audience hall, because I had to be carried by litter-bearers through a tunnel that connected the Palatine to the Oppian, the southern spur of the Esquiline Hill. It was about three hundred passus, and there were inclines, both downhill and uphill. A different palace on a different hill, yet the linking passageways made it all part of the same world, Nero's world, far from the bustle of the world's most crowded city.

The throne room was shiny and new, part of the Golden House that had been continuously under construction since the great fire, now in part deemed fit for habitation. The new palatial complex took up most of the

Oppian. On this spot had once been slums with insulae housing thousands of poor people. Now there was this Imperial chamber, with a vast mural that continued around three sides of the hall depicting the last days of the Trojan War. A huge statue of the Divinitas, with his right arm upraised in a kind of benediction dominated the far wall. I could have sworn I had seen the same statue once in the forum, except that then it had the head of Augustus. Of course, statues' heads are routinely changed when there is a new Emperor, but you would think Augustus would be sacrosanct.

When I arrived, the salutatio had been going on for a little while. A few petitions had been brought on behalf of various traitors; to most people's surprise, Himself had proved merciful, commuting a damnatio ad bestias to a more gentlemanly suicide, and even banishing a few people instead of killing them.

He was at his most magnanimous that morning. He was not properly dressed to be a god, having it seemed, not bothered with makeup or robes.

He waved me over to a throne that was on an equal height to his own. "Come, Poppaea," he said. "Time to dominate our troops."

Epaphroditus, ever the Imperial gatekeeper, gave a signal and two Praetorians in full dress uniform approached. I knew them both, of course. Tigellinus, who had always treated me like some kind of insect ... and Nymphidius, who never bothered to conceal his lust for me.

But I was not the boy they once despised.

Now I was their mistress, whom they still despised, though they could not show it. Instead, they were forced to prostrate themselves before me.

"I trust you are in good health, Empress," Tigellinus said. He didn't realize that I could hear the sound of his gritted teeth.

"I am," I said sweetly. "All healed now." I flashed a smile.

"You are even more beautiful, Divinitas," said Nymphidius, "than you were before your ... accident."

"I should think I would not be the worse for it," I said. I made sure he saw a momentary glower before I smiled again.

Epaphroditus beckoned again and slaves came from within, carrying heavy gilded chests — two slaves to a chest, and even then they were almost too heavy to lift. They opened the chests, which were filled to the brim with gold aurei.

Surely there were not so many gold coins in the world. Each one was worth a hundred sestertii, more than a month's pay for a common legionary. One chest could buy a legion for a year, and the chests kept coming.

"I trust my husband and I will have your loyalty," I said. "Distribute it however you see fit." I knew this meant that Tigellinus and Nymphidius would get the lion's share.

It took the better part of an hour for soldiers to carry away all the gold.

By the time it was all done, the other petitioners had left, for the time allotted for salutatio was long over. Only the two chiefs of the Praetorians remained, standing at attention and waiting to be dismissed by the Emperor.

I got up from my throne and turned to see Nero chuckling.

"What have you done?" I said. "Stripped the gold from the statues of the gods?"

"It's just a loan," he said. "I'll replace it."

Epaphroditus whispered in my ear, "It's not as much as it looks, Divinitas. Or, from another viewpoint, more than it looks. There's been a bit of debasement."

"In the gold?"

"In the silver denarius, Empress. So an aureus can get you more denarii than ever."

The two Praetorians could hear everything we said. I could see they didn't mind about the silver coinage being debased. They were going to pay their underlings in denarii and hang on to the gold themselves. They had become even richer than they'd calculated, for it was the ones below their rank who would get swindled.

"But what if they strip the gods bare?" I said, louder than I should have.

Nero, who had heard me, said, "I'll just raise taxes; Epaphroditus, you'll see to it."

"Divinitas —"

"How's the urine tax going? Sporus's idea — and a very clever one, too. Togas have to stay white, and laundries never go out of business."

"There's been a lot of discontent about that urine tax," said Epaphroditus.

"Riots," Nymphidius said.

"But you've put them down," said Himself.

Nymphidius Sabinus peered at me, while pretending to keep his head bowed. "The Empress has given us a generous donativum," he said. "We shall protect the Empress."

"Excellent," Nero said.

I looked into the Praetorian's eyes. He had that practiced blank look that many courtiers have, so that they won't give themselves away. But though I had been at court only a short time, I saw what flickered beneath that empty gaze. He was pledging to protect *me*. Nero was too self-involved to consider that Nymphidius had not said he would protect the Emperor.

In that moment, I knew there was a plot. A plot hatched in our absence. A plot that probably involved half the people the Emperor called his friends.

I've often said that so much has happened to me, a boy not even twenty. Yes, I am young to have lived through so much. And yet …

Now remember, as you hear out the rest of my story, that Nero Claudius Caesar August Germanicus was no withered, aging pervert like Tiberius, no stuttering old fool like his uncle Claudius. He was younger than the carpenter god of the Chrestianoi. Caligula was that age, too, when they knifed him in the tunnel between the palace and the Circus Maximus.

Nero was barely thirty, and already, I knew, his days were numbered.

Nero had killed, directly or indirectly, those who had truly cared for me. He was all I had left. In his own way he loved me, even though the only way he ever showed love was by inflicting pain. But now I would have to consider survival.

And that unsavory man Nymphidius, with his lascivious sneer and his ill-concealed lust for my body, a man I had always loathed, was offering me a lifeline.

XX

Gaius Julius Vindex

And while we slept, the tide was already turning. The Senate was having a secret meeting to overhaul the taxes ... and the fact that Gaius Julius Vindex, a governor in Gaul, was leading a revolt.

When I awoke, Himself was no longer there. That was unusual; it's normal that the person of highest status in a bed is the last to wake, and finds that everything has been made ready for him.

In one corner of the room, Hylas was folding togas.

"Lucius?" I said softly, expecting that the Divinitas was outside in the private garden. Watering the flowers, perhaps, since he was the only person in the Empire whose urine wasn't taxed. As I sat up, I saw someone else.

Standing at the foot of the bed was the last person I would have expected to see. But as I slowly became aware of things, I realized that her coming was inevitable.

"Actë," I whispered.

"I came as soon as I felt it," she said, "and my feelings never lie." It was true. At every truly key moment in Nero's life, Actë had somehow managed to be present. She lived in shadow, absent from the parties, the orgies, the poetry readings, the arena, and the discussions on strategy, yet she always knew when a moment of crisis was at hand.

I said, "Will this be the last time?"

But I had already divined the answer. From what Vespasian had told me in Greece. From whispers in the corridors in the brief days since our return.

Actë said, "I fear it. I heard everything that happened in Greece. Even what happened to that actor."

The image surfaced in my mind. Lucius Domitius Paris, the greatest actor of our time, flayed alive and flapping in the breeze of sunset while Himself intoned his flawed hexameters to cowed onlookers, even as his most powerful general was in the process of abandoning him. The Emperor declaiming with such mad passion. The actor's skin fluttering. The gorgeous twilight over Olympia. The attar of roses that doused the Divinitas blending with the stench of freshly-killed flesh. I tried to blank my mind, but the nightmare memory would not subside quickly.

"Poor Sporus," Actë said softly. "The things you've seen, the things he had you live through."

She held out a hand and tugged me up from the bed. In a moment, Hylas materialized and was starting to dress me.

"Go away," I said. "I freed you."

But Hylas only laughed as he tied the subligaculum around my loins and slipped a cool silk tunic over my naked body. "Yes, domine," he said, "you freed me."

"Tell them to dress you quickly," Actë said. "Male, I think. Full toga. I think we are going to the Senate."

"Senate? But we're not members," I said.

"And I'm a woman," she said. "Come along. We may not be full members of the Conscript Fathers, but I know where all the peepholes are."

***

There was, not at all to my surprise, a secret room that could be reached through a tunnel, then a back stairwell. It was a low-ceilinged upper room in the Curia Julia; while there was no view of the senatorial chamber, the sound was particularly clear, echoing through a system of pipes that had been engineered for eavesdropping. The Divinitas was already there, and his aspect was grim as he sat on a golden curule, flanked by Epaphroditus, his secretary on one side, and the Praetorian Tigellinus on the other.

Where was Nymphidius? I was he who had said I would be protected in this crisis. Nymphidius wanted something from me, something I knew I could still trade on; to Tigellinus I was as useless as any other pleasure object. I was about to ask someone, but Nero shushed me with a finger to his lips.

"Listen to that one go on!" Nero was muttering.

We heard a quavery old man: "And what is our Divine Emperor doing while Gaius Julius Vindex leads a rebellion in Gaul? Are we to return to the internecine chaos of the interregnum, after a century of this pseudo-monarchy that has stripped the Senate of its rightful authority? Must seven centuries of the Roman Republic end in this nightmare dictatorship?"

Epaphroditus said, "Titus Viridianus. An old fool. I'm surprised he wasn't eliminated in the last purge."

"We can remedy that," Tigellinus said. "It's never too late for a fresh purge."

"Wait," said Epaphroditus.

Tigellinus said, "Indeed. I have the Senate surrounded, as a precaution."

Viridianus was continuing, "Of course it would normally behoove us to send a force to crush this Vindex before it gets out of hand. Yet are there not some people in this chamber who would favor Vindex, who has after all declared his allegiance to General Galba, governor in Spain, a man considered perhaps eminently more sensible as a ruler than our mad poet Emperor?"

"I smell treason," Tigellinus said.

"Let's march right in there and arrest them!" said Himself.

But Epaphroditus said, "Wait, Divinitas, wait." He held up his hand. Surely more senators would condemn themselves if we gave them more time. And they did.

"Didn't you already send money to Galba?" A whiny, wheezy voice. "*And* donated to Nero's triumphal games?"

Another voice: "It doesn't hurt to bet on the green *and* the red. Nero is popular with the mob, and relatively harmless to those of us who stay out of sight. I might just retreat to my new estates in Sicily."

"Sextus Varus," Epaphroditus whispered.

"Estates in Sicily," said Tigellinus. "Something you'd like to add to your holdings, Divinitas?"

"Make a note of it," said Nero. "Would *you* like something in Sicily, dear?" he added, to Actë.

"You will not be rid of me so easily this time," she said.

"Take the estate," said the Divinitas.

"I'll share it with Poppaea, here," she said, and I thought: *That could never have happened if the real Poppaea were here.*

"It's nice to see you two getting along," said the Emperor.

After an hour or so of listening to various senators incriminating themselves, Himself had had enough. "I'm going in," he said. I started to follow, but he motioned me to stay behind. "Just Tigellinus," he said. "The Senate is no place for wives."

"All right," I said. "I'll listen for people whispering behind your back."

The Emperor left the room and so did most of his entourage, including the Praetorians.

The only people who remained in the eavesdropping chamber were Epaphroditus, Actë, and me. Even the slaves had vanished.

With Nero gone, the atmosphere swiftly changed. We didn't speak. We just listened. The condemnatory babble went on for awhile. Occasionally Epaphroditus identified a speaker.

We could hear the tramp of military boots. Nero had reached the Senate chamber and all at once, the hubbub was stilled.

Then I heard the voice of Tigellinus, matter-of-fact, almost bored. "The following members of the Conscript Fathers," he said, "will commit suicide by dawn tomorrow. Titus Viridianus. Publius Claudius Afer. Lucius Sponsianus. Marcus Plautius Niger." Tigellinus droned on. He didn't sound as though he was sentencing people to death; more like a Greek schoolmaster taking roll call in a roomful of inattentive young aristocrats. The list came to an end and he concluded: "A member of the Guard will attend you at your residence in case you need any lessons in how to die like a proper Roman; though I trust there is no one in this august body who doesn't know how to sensibly and expediently commit suicide. The requisite paperwork will be delivered to your residences, along with witness statements that suicide was carried out and thus your heirs will still inherit, as opposed to all you possess being subject to seizure by the Imperial Estate."

"Those documents will have become meaningless come morning," Epaphroditus said.

"True enough," said Actë. "There are perfectly legal ways of invalidating them. Illegible witness signatures ... misspellings ... even just misplacing some scroll or other."

"Yes. Bureaucracy has been getting more and more devious since the Divine Claudius was Emperor," said Epaphroditus. "But there are more direct ways to intervene. For example ..."

Epaphroditus pulled a document from a fold of his tunica.

I had always been told that governing an Empire was about manipulation and ruthless action, but perhaps it was also true that the secretaries, eunuchs and advisors had the ability to override all those traits with obfuscation. But there was more. In Greece Vespasian had taught me that it was the army who ruled the world.

But it wasn't always so. There was also the bureaucracy.

"I have here," Epaphroditus said, "as it happens, a letter from General Gaius Julius Vindex."

"Isn't that treason?" I blurted out, forgetting all I had been learning about keeping my composure.

"You heard Nymphidius," said Nero's trusted freedman, the man who held all the keys to the Empire. "Even if Nero did not. The army pledged its loyalty to *you*, Empress."

Actë began to laugh. And suddenly, Epaphroditus, too, was laughing. Presently, the absurdity of it all was so overwhelming that I too was suppressing laughter.

"It is not as ridiculous as you think," Actë said. "Wasn't it Nero's idea for you to be the one to hand out the donativum? He *planned* this! He thinks, my poor beautiful mad beloved, that when everyone turns against him, *you* will still be foolish enough to want to protect him."

"Me?" I said.

"Yes," Actë said. "Because, beneath all the manufactured drama, *he* is the only reason you exist as a thing of value in the world. And you love him for it."

As always, it was Actë alone who dared speak the truth that was hidden.

XXI

Speaking to Gods

"Don't misunderstand me," Epaphroditus said. "I *love* the Divinitas. More than that; I love the *man*. I have to. I have been his slave; I am now his freedman; I belong to him in a way no one can understand who has not been a slave. As you, Sporus, will always belong to Gaius Petronius Arbiter, even now, when you are Queen of the World."

"Love isn't always about blind devotion," said Actë.

"No, it's not. But it *is* about belonging to another person completely, unconditionally, utterly. My whole life has been about smoothing the journey of Nero's life," said Epaphroditus. "Softening every blow, salving every hurt. There are so few of us. In his journey, we're the cushions in the litter. We soften the bumps in the road. We have helped him to live as beautifully as he could, despite the flaws we all know about. And now, there comes that time when we must help him to die beautifully, too."

I thought, he has found the good even in slavery, which is the darkness at the heart of this luminous civilization; it is the structure that sustains the edifice.

I did not believe any of it. Philosophers turn black to white, and evil to good, all the time, with this nonsense they call logic.

I asked Epaphroditus how we could help Himself to die when dying was probably furthest from his mind.

"We have to ease him into it," he said.

Actë added, "We might even have to do the thing which must not be thought."

Which was, of course, the thing *everyone* in an Imperial court contemplates.

Believe me, for I have lived in four of them and even reigned, after a fashion, in some.

***

In the night, the God made perfunctory attempts to penetrate his Queen. Himself did not succeed and presently he fell into a kind of slumber, twisting, turning, muttering imprecations in his sleep. I could not sleep at all, my mind racing about all the treason whirling around the Imperial court ... including, in a sense, my own.

A few hours before sunrise Himself sat up abruptly, startling me awake as well. "I have to talk to her in person," he mumbled. He sprang from the bed. Slaves emerged from the shadows bearing lamps and clothes. Hylas was in the background rubbing his eyes.

"You have to talk to who?" I said.

"Are you coming?" said the Divinitas.

"Who?" I said, still mentally exhausted from today's revelations.

"Mother, of course," said Nero. "She'll know what to do."

It would have been tactless to point out that the Divinitas had long ago disposed of his mother, so I just told Hylas to go and talk to those standing guard outside the chamber. "Just tell them Himself is going somewhere. Urgently. They'll know what to do."

They did. In the half-dark of the antechamber, a litter was readied, as well as a small guard — nothing ostentatious, just for protection — and Nero paused only for a modicum of makeup, just a simple coating of ghostly white to the face, a touch of kohl for the eyes, a paste of powdered gold for the lips; and he wore only a simple tunica, though as befit his rank it was completely dipped in purple, worth a half-year's wages of a centurion, I guessed. Oh, and a gold tiara in the shape of a laurel wreath, to remind us all that he was the world's universal artist.

All this was prepared with the swiftness of slaves who have no life other than the will of their lord ... and the urgency of knowing their lord might not be long for this world.

Meanwhile, it was Hylas who was taking charge, unnoticed, whispering to the guards the names of whom to summon, who needed to be in attendance. But as no one knew where we were going, I was not sure that he was doing anything useful.

"Watch Hercules," I told him. "Get them to bring him something nice."

"Peacock's brain?"

"A whole peacock."

I was wondering how Nero planned to have any kind of conversation with his mother — even setting aside the fact that she was dead. If he could talk to the dead, would she even want to talk to him ... her own murderer?

In the litter, he did explain where we were going. The litter-bearers, not wanting to appear not to have divined Himself's will, were moving slowly, in order to give the impression they knew where we were going.

I was alone with the God in the litter.

"Tell them to hurry," he said to me. The bearers' footsteps were echoey, and our pathway was sloping downwards. We must be in a tunnel, one of the secret pathways away from the palace.

"Their minds are not as all-seeing as yours, Divinitas," I said. "Let's give them a clue, at least."

"You're being cunning again, my pet," said the Emperor. "Where do *you* think I'll be able to talk to my mother?"

"My first thought would have been the Temple of Capitoline Jove," I said, "since all the Divine Julio-Claudians are with Jupiter now, feasting on ambrosia and on nectar poured by none other than Ganymede ..."

"The only creature in Heaven and Earth who *might* be more beautiful than you," Nero said. "But I hear a *but* coming."

"The Senate hasn't declared Agrippina a goddess," I said.

"Strange, isn't it! That a congregation of senile buffoons has the power to confer a seat on Mt. Olympus, when they can't even organize my piss tax properly."

"So she doesn't have a temple of her own, either, unlike the Divine Augustus," I said. "But gods live in temples, and gods have wives …"

"Uncle Claudius! You *are* clever," said the Emperor.

"The Divine Claudius," I said. "Your Uncle Claudius … he *has* been deified. She might have gone to be with him."

It was dark in the litter; there was just the one lamp lit, and it was sputtering, as the slaves had not had time to refill all the lamps before morning. Yet I could see Himself smile. He liked the fact that I was clever.

"There's more to you than meets the eye," he said. And he ran a finger lightly across my cheek.

The litter was moving more purposefully now, as I made sure to speak loudly enough for them to overhear. The pace picked up. The bearers were moving at a trot. We had emerged from the tunnel, but I did not dare peer through the litter drape. I could hear the clank of horse-drawn carts, so I knew it was not yet dawn.

The litter moved more swiftly now.

Familiar smells of the eleventh hour of night: bread baking, sausages and fish being grilled in the open waiting to serve thousands of breakfasts for people on their way to the Forum or the baths. The litter-bearers were moving so quickly now that the smells and sounds were blending into chaos. I could hear our guards quirting people out of the way.

And now we were moving steeply uphill. The Caelian Hill, I knew. You could see it from the private garden of the chamber I shared with the God. The litter angled upward. I heard the trickle of water on marble. I slipped back into Nero's arms. Then the litter righted itself, and stopped. We stepped out. Gazing across the city I could see the sunrise, and the secret garden

We stood in an open space, with trees, columns on three sides, and, where the Caelian rose, a marble wall with a complex web of fountains and waterfalls and statues of nymphs, some spewing water from their lips, others catching it in their hands or outstretched arms; water channels crisscrossed the floor.

"Look," said the Emperor. He pointed across the valley and all the way up to where if I squinted, we could make out the wall around our private garden, angling out from the hillside. I imagined beyond the wall Hercules skulking among the herms and flowers. "It's us," said Nero.

"Actually, we're down here," I said.

"No, we're not. I mean, yes, but up there ... that's the *idea* of us, you see. This great and sprawling empire, and at the summit, it's us, you see. There we stand, the poet-emperor-god, in an eternal embrace with his beautiful boy-girl-wife."

Sunrise in my eyes; I squeezed them shut. Very suddenly, a tear came. "I'm losing you," I said softly.

"You won't lose me."

"Your mother did," I said, and immediately regretted it.

"You're not my mother," he said. Decades of rage concealed in his soft utterance.

Then came a voice from within, thundering with authority, "But *I* am."

Damnatio Memoriae · 144

XXII

The Priestess of Claudius

A priestess stood in front of the waterfall. She looked to be the type that had been dedicated to the gods since childhood, and had known no other life until now. She was wrinkled, shrunken, wrapped in a cloth covered with ancient bloodstains. She was wet, too, having burst through the curtain of water.

"Lucius," she shrieked, "Lucius, Lucius, you've come looking for me at last."

Nero made to follow her into the gushing water. I held him back. "Be careful, Lucius," I said. "She isn't really Agrippina."

"But she is. I'd know her voice anywhere."

Two acolytes in white tunicae emerged and dragged her back behind the waterfall, and in her place stood a priest. Imposing, with a white beard, every inch what one imagines a representative of the gods to look like.

"Divinity," said the priest, "Agrippina's shade appears to have possessed one of our priestesses. You may speak to her, but it is also possible that what possesses her is just some kind of madness."

We could still her shrieks from behind the rushing of the waterfall.

"It's the gods who send madness," said Nero, "as Euripides tells us ... *I've driven them from their wits, and from their homes* ... that's what the God Bacchus did."

"And in the same play, the prophet also says, *There is no cure for madness. The cure itself is madness,*" said the priest.

"I see you know the classics," said my husband.

"Priests are not uneducated," said the representative of the God Claudius. "When your uncle lived in the world, he loved knowledge. He wrote histories of the Etruscans, and studied the past with great attention."

"Perhaps not Euripides," said Nero.

"No," said the priest. "That would be my personal passion. It was with great interest that I followed the news of your victory in Greece. I must admire you, Divinitas, for your victory, against all odds, in the wrong year."

"And at such sacrifice," said Nero.

"I'm sure he suffered greatly," said the priest, making Himself realize that he knew exactly what had happened with Nero's rival Paris.

"I atone every day," Himself said. "I torment myself through the night. I weep tears of blood."

"Perhaps not quite enough," said the priest.

"How so?"

"There are many kinds of sacrifice, but in general, Divinitas, they are concerned with avoidance — you send an envoy to the land of death — a pigeon, a goat, a snow-white bull — one rarely sends oneself."

"You mean I need to sacrifice myself? How then should I return with an answer?"

"Ah, yes," the priest said, "a paradox."

"Lucius," I said, "I don't think he means it literally."

"I think he does," said the Emperor. "He wants me to be like the god of the Chrestianoi, you see. Redeeming the world by sacrificing himself."

"I didn't know," I said, "that you knew anything about their philosophy."

"Oh, Epaphroditus keeps me informed. If you're going to execute a few thousand people, you should study them a bit." He turned to the priest. "A drop of blood," he said, "and I speak to my mother for one hour."

"A single drop?"

"It's the blood of a god," I said quickly. "And you don't know how squeamish he is. I'll have to prick him myself."

"A quarter of an hour, then."

The priest bade the Divinitas step through the waterfall, and put out an arm to block my path. But the Emperor said, "No, no, the Empress never leaves my side. And she needs to take my blood."

The water rushed only for a minute. We were through and in some kind of cave. A few torches flickered in brackets in the rock, but you could hardly see through thickets of frankincense.

The Divine Claudius, in effigy, loomed above us, rising from a little dais in the center of the cave. I had heard him called a stuttering fool, but as a god, he was imposing. There was an altar, and a brazier with more incense. On the altar the old woman writhed. "Lucius!" she shrieked. "Don't you miss me?"

Then, after a frightening spasm, she collapsed upon the altar, spent, whimpering.

"The blood," the priest said.

I led my master by the hand to where the priestess lay. I unhooked the fibula that held my garment in place. It had a dolphin design, for it came all the way from Britannia.

I stood naked next to my God. I took his hand and stabbed the fibula into the fleshiest part of his palm. He yelped in a most ungodlike manner, and I touched the bleeding spot to the priestess's forehead. She twitched, then was still.

"Just like Uncle Claudius, this entire operation," Nero said. "He wasn't a real Emperor, just an idiot in purple robes."

The priestess sat up. "You silly boy!" she spat. Himself was so taken aback he did not answer, but snatched away his hand and stepped back. "Claudius was no fool. But *you* are!"

From a few paces' distance, I watched the woman transform. It seemed she could control her very cheek muscles. Her face was quivering and re-forming. She was becoming another person entirely, and Himself, the Dominus of the Cosmos, was quaking.

"Don't say I'm a fool," he murmured.

"I gave you the throne," she said, "and you had me killed."

"Killed? You're right here!" said Nero.

"And *you*, child, are right here," she hissed, pointing to her own womb. "You want to see the place that engendered such a monster as yourself?"

With that she threw herself back on the altar and launched into a terrifying parody of childbirth. She tore at her garments. Her dugs slapped against withered flesh. She whimpered and shrieked and clawed the air. Himself watched in awe, completely convinced. He stood beside her, held her hand, whimpered in tandem with the priestess. It would have been comical were it not so terrifying.

"You're tearing me apart!" she screamed. "I'm birthing a god!"

"Mama!" he cried — and it looked as though he were trying to crawl inside her. I could not look away. He had utterly infantilized himself while his surrogate mother flailed at the air. Clouds of incense billowed. I was choking. I turned away, retching.

When I looked up again, he had wrapped his arms about her and appeared to be attempting to suckle.

"There, there," the priestess said. "Perhaps you *have* killed me, but there's still enough of me left for you to love."

"Are you waiting for me?" he said.

"What else is there to do here?" she said. "You didn't have me made a god, and now it's too late."

"I can command the Senate."

"You can't even command your wife."

"Poppaea!" He reached behind his back, clawing the air until I went to hold his hand. Then he pulled me into the bone-chilling embrace of the old woman. "Poppaea," he said, "you'll tell the Senate. You'll still have influence. Nymphidius will protect you."

It was likelier that Nymphidius would rape me to death, I thought. But I only said, "Yes, Lucius. I'll tell the Senate."

"And me, too. Don't forget me. I have to be a god. Otherwise … they pursue you." He stared wildly about, seeing creatures no one else could see. "To the ends of the earth, to the edge of death."

"Who chases you, Lucius?" I said.

He cringed. He clung to the simulacrum of his mother. I realized that he was being tormented by those who drive matricides mad, the Furies.

"They're not here. How could they be? I didn't kill … her. Look. She's still here."

"There, there," the priestess said. "I'm here. But you have to go."

"My Empress will make you a goddess. I promise."

"You too, my dearest," I said, and kissed him on lips that tasted of vomit.

"You'll make sure I can be with Uncle Claudius?"

"Yes," I said.

"I'm not mad," said Nero. "I know you're not Poppaea. I killed Poppaea. I killed my mother. The Furies are standing all around me and I smell their rancid breath. No, you're not my wife. You're not my mother. You are all phantoms."

More incense thickened the close air. I watched the master of the world weeping in the arms of the priestess. I watched and felt nothing.

And as he wept, I too felt drawn into a vision of my own. The cave, it seemed, grew larger, darker, the flickers of light fewer and farther between, until it seemed I stood in a place I recognized from other dreams I had had ... I was in the underworld again. I knew I was there, because I could feel the shade of my dead friend Hyacinth, and he was speaking to me in the language of our childhood.

"He thinks he's going to fly up, up, up to the height of high Olympus," he said in an eerie singsong. It was a sound I dimly remembered from childhood, some shaman intoning against the background of the sea. "He's not going to fly fly, fly. He's going to fall, fall, fall. But he will still rule."

And then I saw what I'd already seen in other visions. The throne of the king of the dead, and on that throne Nero, his eyes piercing me with a savage cold light.

"Go to him," Hyacinth said. "You don't have a choice. No man conquers death."

Hyacinth's chanting rose in pitch until it became am wordless keening. Dead youths were dressing me in black robes.

The King of Death spoke to me. "Persephone," he said.

I walked slowly towards him. More dead souls were gathering, strewing my way with wilted flowers. The Lord of the Dead gazed upon me with eyes of infinite sadness, yet I saw no tears. The dead do not weep.

"Lucius," I said softly. The vision faded and I saw that the living *do* weep.

When the Emperor had wept until he was spent, he sat up slowly, gathering his wits. He looked from side to side, and it seemed that his apparitions of the Furies were fading.

He looked at me, too, and whispered, "Persephone."

I thought of the ill-omened intaglio I had given him in Greece.

In Greece we had both had a vision in the temple, but we had not shared the same vision.

But I knew that this time he had seen me in the land of death. As queen.

So I was not his plaything, but Death herself, Death who comes to all, like a mother, like a lover. I smiled a little, hoping to give some comfort. But the Emperor was past consoling.

And presently they came to take Himself to the place that had been chosen for his suicide.

Damnatio Memoriae · 154

XXIII

A Place to Die

We had arrived in Rome in a triumphal convoy, fresh from Himself's great victory in Greece. We departed in the back of an oxcart, in secrecy. The sun was still rising, but we only had moments to leave the city, because of the ban on animal-drawn vehicles during the daylight hours. Hylas was driving, since there was no one of lowlier status with us to do anything menial.

We left through the Esquiline Gate, the nearest, erected by the God Claudius himself, as Nero told me, in a murmur, peering from an opening in the canvas cover of the cart.

"Why can't they just send a professional?" Nero said, shaking his head. "A gladiator. Someone to do it quickly and painlessly. Decapitation's almost instant. I could hardly cut off my own head."

He seemed almost flippant about our world tumbling down around us. He was cheerful, even, especially after days of moodiness and the big shouting match with the priestess-mother surrogate.

Epaphroditus, leaning over from the passenger seat, drew back the drape and said, "My Lord, it's customary to do this one yourself."

"It *is* called *suicide*, I suppose," the Emperor said meekly.

"Where are we going?" I asked Epaphroditus.

"There's a place prepared," he said. "It is only a few miles beyond the walls, but it is safe. It belongs to Phaon, one of the Emperor's freedmen and a loyal client. No one will intrude."

By that, I was sure he meant that the Praetorians were already aware that the Emperor would finish the final chapter there. I was sure that, eventually, they would intrude, after allowing a decent interval to perform the act. We had at most a few days.

The road was crowded. "Can't you make them go faster?" I said to Hylas.

"They're oxen, domine," he said.

They were intolerably sluggish, and more so as we turned at the first milestone to the north, moving bumpily through mud and stones. It took almost until midday to reach Phaon's villa, though it was a mere four miles from from the city gates. Even though there was no one around us, we did not lower the awning, or there would have been no shade.

"It's only June," Nero said, "and it's already sticky. Let's get it over with. I shall be glad to have managed to miss the stench of summer sweat in the city."

There was an olive grove where a little Cupid was set up for lovers to worship at. A pair of dead doves lay entwined on the altar, and behind the shrine we found a paved path at last, though somewhat overgrown with weeds.

The villa itself was nothing much. A statue of the Emperor stood in the entrance hall. There were no lares or penates, because, as a freedman, Phaon didn't really have proper ancestors as such. In Rome, only Romans count.

Like all villas, this one had an atrium, a portico, and side rooms. Epaphroditus led us to a chamber with no windows. The wall was painted with a sylvan mural, so we did not feel hemmed in. The mural was new, and overbright; things in the chamber did not belong together; mismatched vases, a tapestry the wrong color and so on; Phaon's taste would not have pleased my late patronus.

***

This Phaon had come ahead, and was there to greet us along with another freedman named Neophytus. They were hard to tell apart, except that Neophytus did not speak.

Phaon greeted the Emperor at the doorway, prostrating himself. "The Senate's gone and done it," he said. He did not dare meet Nero's gaze but spoke to me instead. "The Divinitas has been pronounced Damnatio Memoriae. His name is to be erased from every monument, every inscription; his statues to be taken down; his effigy no longer stamped on legitimate Roman coinage."

"We are not to be gods, then?" Nero said to me.

"There was no such sentence passed on the Empress," Phaon said. "The Senate thinks the Lady Poppaea Sabina may yet have a role to play." He said this without apparent irony, even knowing who I really was. We inhabited an imaginary universe, after all. A man was a God and a boy was an Empress.

We half carried, half dragged the Emperor to a couch that had known better days; the rose-leaf stuffing was leaking from a torn corner. A girl brought the Divinitas a kylix of wine. The Emperor sniffed and rejected it with a baleful glare. The slave scurried away.

"No wine. I want to face this moment with utter clarity," he said. "What an artist dies in me! I want a final death-song that will rank with the last words of the most beautiful heroes of antiquity."

"My Lord," Epaphroditus said, "don't do Niobe again. That was ill-omened."

"Niobe lost her children," said Nero. "But today, my children are losing *me*."

"Hylas," I said, "bring water." I dismissed the other hangers-on; Nero only wanted to have people around him he knew, people he believed loyal. Some would have called us sycophants. Yet I think everyone in the room truly loved Nero, on some level.

I am sure of it because of what happened in this room.
***

At first it was as if nothing at all was going on. The Divine Nero sipped water from a glass krater. We waited. It seemed that the air itself thickened, began to weigh down on us.

Epaphroditus finally started to say something, but the Emperor held up his hand. "I'm writing a new song," he said quietly.

We waited. And after a few more sips of water, he began to sing, without lyre or other instrument, in a dulcet falsetto.

We stand on the stairway that leads to the gates of Olympus, he sang, then stopped. And again he started: *We stand on the steps ...* and stopped again. There were tears in his eyes.

"They love me," he said softly. "The people love me. I just have to show myself."

"The Senate doesn't," said Epaphroditus. "The army doesn't."

"Is there any pain?" said the Emperor.

"Not if you do it quickly," Epaphroditus said, though I sensed he was lying.

"And Actë, Actë ... why isn't she here?"

"She is on her way, Divinitas," Phaon said, without much conviction.

"Oh, look," said Nero, pointing at the mural, "an enchanted forest. Such awful taste you have, Phaon."

"We can't all be Petronius Arbiter," Phaon said.

We stand on the stairway that leads to Olympus, the Emperor sang again, changing the words a little to improve the scansion. Each line ended with an elegantly ornamented melisma. We listened to him for a few moments, and he abruptly stopped.

"The Muse is reticent today," he said. "Are we surprised?"

He sat, fidgeting, called for more wine. Finally he said, "I don't have a song in me, Poppaea."

"Maybe you don't have to sing it aloud," I said softly. "Maybe you can just think it."

"And you'll hear it on the wind, my darling," he said.

"I'll hear it on the wind."

"On the wind."

"*Like a mountain wind —*"
"*As it swoops down upon an oak tree —*"
"*Love shook my heart,*" I said.

Ah, Sappho! Centuries-old words I once heard on the lips of Petronius, who owned me, yet never treated me like a *thing*. I had been Petronius's muse, but I was not Nero's.

"Thank you for reminding me," Nero said, "that while I tower above you all, while I am your sheltering sky, your Divinitas, there is a high Divinitas that I must look to."

As expected, we all protested that no, we believed in no higher power than Nero Claudius Caesar Augustus Germanicus; he was our only world; he was our protector, the love of our lives. We said this, repeatedly and with a desperate desire to have him believe us, knowing full well that Epaphroditus had been in communication with those who planned the Emperor's downfall.

"It's fine," he went on. "Do not weep for me. I will await you in my Imperial palace in the sky." I did not remind him that he would not be in Olympus unless the Senate were to enact his deification. Rome has created so pervasive a bureaucracy that it encompasses the very gods. "But," he went on, and he pulled me down to his lap, and covered my face with soft kisses, "I want *you* to do it. These people around me … perhaps they'll feast on my corpse as soon as I'm gone. *You* won't. You are my one true wife. You will reign with me on Olympus."

"You want me to …"

"Give him a sword," said Himself, waving at slaves who were not there.

"No, Lucius," I whispered. "Come on, I don't know swords. I was trained as a delicatus, not a gladiator."

"You'll do as I tell you!" he said with abrupt harshness.

I recoiled. Not missing a beat, he continued, with infinite tenderness, "Because you are the only one who really loves me."

"Your mother…"

"I killed her! I killed Poppaea! I killed them all! Now … you, Sporus, you … kill me. I order it."

Phaon held up a monstrous gladius; I would not have even had the strength to lift it, let alone wield it. I shook my head. Presently it was Hylas who thrust a dagger into my hand. It was almost a toy, with a jewelled pommel and a phallus incised upon the hilt, perhaps something you'd play with at the lupanar.

"My beautiful boy-wife," said the Emperor, "make love with me one last time."

I held the poignard in my left hand, and with my right I stroked Nero's cheek. He had not had time for his morning attentions. I touched stubble, mingled with tears. I kissed him. He pulled at the fibula that held my clothes together and they slid to the floor. He drew me towards him. "I belong to you," he whispered. "You have my leave to penetrate me." The ultimate abasement of a Roman, something never to be done in front of others, not even freedman.

"You know I can't anymore," I said.

He unfastened his own robes. I sat in his lap, my cheeks against his cheeks. He was entirely flaccid, stripped of manhood. As *I* had been since before we went to Greece. "I can't," I repeated again.

He guided my left hand so that the point of the blade touched his lower abdomen. "Yes, you can. See? A God can do anything. I took away your manhood. Now, in my last moments in this earth, I've made you hard again."

"My Lord —"

Was this delusion? Did he *know* he was weaving a fabric of fantasy, or had he already entered the unreal world? "Push into me, my love," said Nero.

"I don't want to hurt you, Lucius," I said.

"Oh, so considerate!" he said. "But you can't hurt me anymore."

He hugged me savagely to him, forcing the dagger in deeper. He moaned. And I too moaned, not in desire but in sheer terror. He squeezed me again and again, each time crying out, and then there came a moment when the illusion must have been shattered, he was screaming in pain now, and I was trying to disentangle myself but the dagger sank deeper, blood was spurting now, gushing on to my hands and chest, and still he clung to me as I slipped and slid on the slick blood.

Suddenly I felt rough hands seizing my shoulders.

"You stupid boy! Can't you get anything right?" It was Nymphidius Sabinus. He pushed me to one side. He sliced into the Emperor's chest with a single stroke of his sword. The God slumped to the floor. Epaphroditus and the others were babbling, screaming.

I stood there, naked and bloody, shivering though the room was intolerably hot.

More Praetorians entered the chamber now. Nero's freedmen prostrated themselves, expecting to be killed. Nymphidius told them to be silent. The Praetorians lifted up the dead God and placed him on the couch. Others cleaned the blood.

I still stood there, numb. I was not thinking that my world had ended, that I had lost everything I had so recently gained. As I gazed on the face of the man who had once owned my mind and my body, I did not even feel relief.

Nymphidius gave one of his soldiers a brief nod. That man decapitated Phaon and Neophytus in quick succession.

"Enough," Nymphidius said. "Nero's secretary may prove useful. He'll have access to all the records. Can't run an empire without a creature like him."

We heard Hylas whimpering in a corner.

"A pretty slave," Nymphidius said. "Give him to the centurions."

"I'm free," said Hylas softly.

"No one is truly free," Nymphidius said.

"You know your Euripides," I said.

"Ah! The Empress deigns to speak!" said Nymphidius. "You know, I'm not a barbarian, though you snubbed me at every turn."

"Hylas was my slave," I said. "I freed him. The appropriate documents have been properly drawn up."

"And if I were to say that the documents have been ... mislaid?" Nymphidius said. "Would you vouch for his freedom?

"I would."

"At what price?"

Nymphidius looked at me. I was naked, soaked in blood. I do not know how I summoned up any semblance of dignity, but somehow, I managed it.

"What you can take," I said, "take. You will not take my soul." I stared him down. Nymphidius wanted me in that very moment. I saw it in his eyes. Yet he stopped short of helping himself to the spoils of usurpation.

"I am impressed," he said. "An Empress's virtue, for the life of a slave. I would have been happy to pay far more, you know."

"Do you mean to take the throne?" I said.

"Tigellinus is off to battle Vindex. I'm the only leader of the Praetorians in Rome, and you know that it's the army who chooses the Emperor."

"Isn't General Galba marching on Rome? Could Vindex not cross the Rubicon too? How long do you think you could hold power for?"

"I have you," he said. Then, to Hylas: "You! Slave or ex-slave, whatever … take the Empress to the bath. Make sure she is cleaned up, and clothe her in whatever finery this sorry household may possess." Then to one of his men he said, "Ride to Rome and kidnap the High Priest from the Temple of Jupiter Optimus Maximus. Get these bodies disposed of, and have the slaves decorate this villa for a nuptials."

It seemed that I was going to remain Empress for a little while longer.

Damnatio Memoriae · 166

XXIV

Imperatrix Reddux

Nymphidius, you say. What do you mean, Nymphidius? There's no Nymphidius among the ones who seized imperium this year.

How do you even remember all their names?

Galba. Galba was next.

I barely knew Galba. A great general, I've heard. I saw him. He barely glanced at me, And he had no animosity toward me. Didn't waste a single thought on me, unlike Nymphidius.

Nymphidius had always been obsessed with me, as I've told you before. I had haunted Nymphidius's dreams, and I did not even know it.

And now, ripped from Nero's fatal embrace, my Emperor barely cold, I was to be married again … to this same Nymphidius.

***

My toilette was cursory. I lay in the bath for barely an hour, with Hylas my only attendant, for Phaon's household was being rounded up and catalogued for auction. Indeed, the water was lukewarm, because there were no slaves in the basement to keep the fires going. I was shivering. Phaon had a full-service private bath, but the frigidarium and the caldarium were the same temperature … tepid.

As I lay in the water I tried to empty my mind. So much hatred, bloodshed, so many plots and counterplots! If the water had been warmer, at least … unable to think, I rose abruptly and went to a lectus where Hylas anointed me with perfumed olive oil, and tenderly scraped my soft skin with a strigil. This was better than the water, Hylas understood every inch of my body as well as his own. If I still had my manhood, his ministrations would surely have aroused me. And yet …

Even unmanned, a felt an echo of the man I could have been, a silky warmth spreading outward from my loins. I did not feel desire, but I did feel Hylas's unquestioning love. That is what I told myself, yet in spite of what I had become, I did feel a twinge, an unexpected stirring. Hylas giggled.

"You didn't lose it *all*, domine," he said.

"I'm not your master," I said.

"If you ever weren't," he said, "I'd die."

"Well," I said, "at least you've mastered the Latin subjunctive." I felt cold for desire to linger. Seeing me shiver, Hylas rubbed the oil harder, then brought a woolen to cover me. I sat up and let Hylas apply some perfunctory makeup; a little lead paint, some kohl for my eyes, a touch of crimson for my lips; I looked like a statue of Venus that has been in the sun too long.

Presently, some very timid slaves came in to dress me, their eyes downcast. They may have been told they could be crucified at any moment. From elsewhere in the house, I could hear unmistakable sounds of people being killed, and the tramp of soldiers' caligae.

Still, these attendants had skills. I do not know if Phaon had a wife; but there were plenty of serviceable women's clothes in the home. They were not the softest, and there wasn't any silk, but there was a stola of linen and a woollen palla edged with some kind of fur. They found me some gold bracelets and a necklace of baroque pearls.

"Your mistress's?" I asked them. They did not respond.

Hylas said, "They told me she hasn't been seen in days, domine."

One of the girls whispered, "She went to her relatives in Gaul."

They held up a mirror. I was hardly the image of an Empress, but then this wedding was going to be a joke as well.

I was right. There were several high-ranking priests present, and a few doves were sacrificed, a few words were said, and I repeated, for the second time in my short life, the magic formula that made me Nymphidius's wife, *Ubi tu Gaius, ibi ego Gaia...*

There was no feast. Nymphidius scooped me up and carried me to the cubiculum. He threw me down on the cubile and began to rip off my tawdry wedding garments. When I struggled, he slapped my face, left and right. I bit my tongue.

"Nymphidius," I said, "I've been a slave. I know how to be raped."

Not to utter a word. Not to cry out for fear of exacerbating the violence. To become nothing. To be no one. To become one with the furniture.

"Whore," Nymphidius said.

My tunica tore in his hand.

"I've watched you for so long. Even when you were nothing, you looked down on me. And when you became Nero's, you made me feel worthless as a dog. You, and everyone else. It's always Tigellinus this, Tigellinus that! Tigellinus, handsomer, crueler, more ruthless, more vicious. I'm the second most powerful man in the Empire, and you didn't offer me one scrawny buttock. That is going to change now. You may think I need you to make my rule legitimate. And yes! Your false pedigree is going to hand me my throne. It doesn't mean you're not my wretched little strumpet."

He shoved me hard, keeping me pinned. He bore down on me, ready to penetrate. I tensed. I tried to be far away. He can't have my soul, I told myself.

"Tomorrow morning I will march into the senate with you by my side," he said. "They won't laugh at me anymore."

With one hand he pushed my face down into the cushions. At least I wouldn't have to look at him. I squeezed my eyes shut. Images of being "broken in" on the pirate ship rushed unbidden to the surface of my memory. *I'm not going to scream,* I told myself over and over. I felt Nymphidius lower himself onto me, the hairs on his chest slick against my back, reeking of sweat and perfume. I tensed. I could feel him rear up now, could feel him probing me, getting ready to thrust.

"You love this," he whispered.

I did not speak and slapped me again. He probably wanted me to whimper. I would not give him any satisfaction.

"Poppaea! Sporus!" he cried out. "Poppaea! Sporus! My Empress! My slave!" Crudely, cruelly, knowing he could as much pain as he wanted to, he began to push himself into me.

I'm not going to scream, I told myself again.

Then I heard footsteps. I heard the swish of metal slicing through the air. Blood drenched the back of my head, ran all over me. I screamed at last, a scream of sheer terror and desolation.

Then I wrenched my face away from the cubile and saw Nymphidius's leering head, a knuckle's breadth away from my face. Blood was gushing from the severed neck. The rest of him had rolled onto the mosaic stones.

I went on screaming now, unbottling all the terror I had shoved deep down into my psyche for years and years. I sat up.

Praetorians stood around me, not staring, not caring. One was sheathing his sword.

For the second time that day, I was naked and bloody, in front of indifferent strangers.

Then a man in a toga entered the room. The soldiers all saluted him. One of them took away the head, and sat me up straight. The blood was sticky on my face, my arms, my back and chest.

"Thank the Gods you're alive," said the man. "I've pined for you every moment that I was in Lusitania."

I did not recognize him at first. But I knew who he was.

"Am I *your* Empress now?" I asked softly. It seemed an unlikely destiny for this man, whom I had known to be completely under his wife's thumb, and whom Nero had treated more or less like a human carpet.

"No, no," said Marcus Salvius Otho, first husband of Poppaea, the man who enjoyed women so little that he once needed me in his bed in order to satisfy his wife, the most beautiful woman in the Empire. "Get dressed. We'll travel together."

"Are we going back to the Senate? Are *you* going to claim the throne?"

"Not at all," he said. "We'll take Nero's body back and have him properly taken care of. After that, we are riding north, to meet General Galba on his way to the city and to make sure we are seen to be his allies. We have to make sure we are not on any proscription list."

"General Galba?"

"Yes. The army has declared him the new Emperor."

Damnatio Memoriae · 174

XXV

OTHO

"Leave Nero here," Otho said as we prepared to leave. For while I had had a wedding on the grounds of this villa, and had almost been raped in the main cubiculum, there was still a room that held the bodies of Nero, his two freedmen, and assorted slaves whom the Praetorians had seen fit to slay. Their bodies were piled up around the late God's, as though the Emperor were holding court to an entourage of corpses.

"Shouldn't we take him back to Rome, offer him up for a proper funeral?" I said.

"Why? He was the most hated man in the world. People will think we are of the Nero faction, and we'll be Circus-fodder."

Otho told us to leave the dead Emperor right where he had died. We had all been instructed not to mention that he had not *exactly* committed suicide. Murdering an Emperor was a crime, after all, no matter how well-intentioned. Suicide was a matter of dignity, of being truly Roman.

"I still don't understand why we can't take the body back," I said to Otho.

"It seems Nymphidius didn't tell you everything," he

said. "The reason the damnatio was enacted was that Nymphidius informed the Senate that the Emperor was in flight, on his way to Egypt."

"So they think he's still alive?"

"Yes. As soon as they pronounced the damnatio, the news arrived that General Galba had defeated the traitor Vindex in battle. Nymphidius thought *he'd* be declared Emperor, but as soon as the Senate heard that Galba had the army, they made *him* Emperor, and he's on his way to Rome now. With several legions to back him up. No one minds marching on Rome any more, not since Julius Caesar crossed the Rubicon. But Galba is still days away, and Nymphidius assumed that with *you* on his arm, he could assume the principate before Galba arrived."

"But I'm on *your* arm now," I said.

"Yes, you are, my darling," he said. "I've dreamed of this day ever since Nero took you from me." I did not remind him that it was Poppaea the Divinitas took, not Petronius's little slave, and that Poppaea did not exactly resist abduction.

"And why don't *you* want to be Emperor?" I asked him.

"You know what I'm like," Otho said, and I truly felt sorry for him; he took me in his arms, blood and all, and kissed me. It was not unwelcome, because Otho was one of the few people with whom I possessed the upper hand. He loved me, or rather, he loved Poppaea, and she spoke to him, in a sense, through me. I kissed him back. We were both covered in blood now, and it was at that moment that Actë arrived, too late for the tragic trilogy. At least she caught the comedic satyr-play that was the dénouement of Nero's so-called suicide.

She rushed into the room and flung herself on Nero's

body. She was weeping loudly, making something of a display of extravagant grief, crying out "Lucius, Lucius," beating her breast. This was not like her.

"Actë, you're too late," Otho said. "And if you carry on so, your life may be in danger."

"What does my life matter?"

"No one wants to be associated with a hated despot," Otho said.

Epaphroditus was hovering. Perhaps he was still in a state of shock at not having been summarily executed.

"Take care of her," I said to him.

"Yes, Divinitas," he said.

***

At first Otho wanted me to follow him on horseback, but that was I skill I had never learned. So once again I found myself clambering into a covered cart, with only Hylas for company; Otho rode in front, and a handful of Praetorians, and we set off down the pathway, away from the house, where the God of Rome was being mourned by a concubine, a freedman, and some dead slaves.

We had barely reached the gates of Phaon's estate when we heard people shouting. Beyond the portal a mob was forming. I could hear murmurs, curses. At first I could not make out what they were saying, but it sounded ominous.

"What's going on?" I said. Hylas, peering through the drapery, said, "They're not letting us through, domino. They're throwing vegetables at the Praetorians."

The crowd were chanting Nero's name. "Where's Nero? Where's Nero?" They were shouting, "We want our Emperor!"

Otho rode up to the cart and said, "We'll need to get

back inside. I'll have the guards clear the mob first."

"I thought you said he was the most hated man in the world," I said.

"He was," Otho said. "Everyone says so."

"That means you've never listened to the mob. If you had, you would have known that the people loved him."

"But he killed people! He was a sexual monster — look what he did to you! He killed the perfectly innocuous Chrestianoi! He even taxed our piss!"

It wasn't just vegetables. I heard rocks clattering against the walls of the estate.

"You said everyone hated Nero," I said, "but you were wrong. Only the Senate hated him. And in Rome, it's the mob that counts."

Otho did not appear to know what to do, even though he had arrived on the scene of Nero's suicide, and had already overseen the execution of a potential usurper. Or at least, had not forbidden the Praetorians to dispose of Nymphidius. But he wasn't really running things. I realized that someone had to make decisions, and that Otho was, now as much as before, a ditherer.

"Hylas," I said, "straighten my robes and fix my makeup. I need to look like Nero's Empress." Hylas brushed me down and refastened my fibula. I got down from the cart.

Otho said, "Oh, no, Poppaea dearest. We need to keep you safe. You are precious. The most precious thing in the world."

"The mob may want to throw rocks at you all the way to the gates of the city," I said. "But they're not going to stone their Empress."

Otho started to protest, but I said only, "Uncover the

cart. I am going to play the role Nero gave me."

"They'll kill you!" Otho said.

"And bring the Emperor."

Some of the soldiers pulled down the awning and someone ran back to the house and returned with a sedile. I got back on and sat enthroned. Hylas sat at my feet. I wasn't Cleopatra on her golden barge, but I needed to carry myself like a Queen. Presently a few slaves came with the the body of Nero, along with Actë and Epaphroditus. Actë continued her ostentatious grieving while Epaphroditus walked with head bowed; I could not tell what thoughts he was having, though I guessed he was most concerned with survival.

We formed a new convoy now,

"Now lead the way," I told Poppaea's ex-husband.

Feeling far more trepidation than I let on, I waved imperiously at the guards. They opened the gates. I saw the crowd, heard jeers and catcalls and demands for the Emperor to appear.

But when I stood up, with the body of my husband decked in Imperial purple in front of me, those who saw fell silent. The silence rippled down the road; I could see people standing, as far as the eye could see, but slowly the crowd was parting, moving to either side of the Appian Way.

A single cry: "Long live the Empress Poppaea Augusta Sabina!"

There came an echo, then another, and another.

And then it seemed the whole crowd erupted.

In that moment, I held more power than anyone in the entire world.

Damnatio Memoriae · 180

XXVI

THE HOUSE OF PETRONIUS

But I knew it was not to be for long.

All the way to the city, it was as though I had been awarded a triumph. When we passed through the gates, the streets narrowed. Crowds crammed the side of the street, pressed into doorways, peering from upper stories and rooftops. The Praetorians, the only military allowed to set foot in the city without Senatorial permission, preceded and followed my cart.

I could not help noting that they were cheering for me, and for Nero, but not for Otho, who turned to left and right and made acknowledging gestures in spite of this.

As we moved towards the Forum and the Curia Julia, the atmosphere changed. Cheering was sporadic. The crowd was better dressed and more sparse. Rich women out with their slaves, coming from dressmakers or jewellers. Men coming from the baths or on their way to symposia. The lupanaria would open later and the patrons of the day would be replaced by the surreptitious traffic of the night.

The sun would set soon. The Senate would normally have gone home by now, since Senate sessions by law had to end by nightfall, but Otho had sent a messenger ahead. When our procession entered the Forum, there was no more cheering. People stood and watched us, dull-eyed, sullen.

There came the solemn pounding of a tympanum. Ahead of us, in the front portico of the Curia Julia, standing behind the colonnade, a man was slowly beating the drum, while alongside came the cacophonous braying of bucinae. They had not managed to get together a decent orchestra for the Emperor's homecoming; the music would have been better on a slow day at the Circus. Nor did it blend well with the bleating and breast-beating of Actë. Deprived of her reason for existing, she had become powerless, pitiful.

We were met at the steps by the consul Tiberius Silius Italicus, who was the only presiding officer in the Senate that day. His co-consul, Publius Galerius Trachalus, was already on the road to greet General Galba.

As the drums pounded and the bucinae wailed, a litter borne by a dozen unmatched slaves emerged from the huge bronze doors of the Curia Julia, and more slaves emerged to lift Nero's body, which had mostly been swabbed clean and was wrapped in a fresh purple cloak, and to transfer it to the litter; the bearers then carried it through the doors, which clanged shut. And that was the last I was to see of Himself, the Master of the World, my tormentor, my benefactor, my lover.

Italicus began to regale me in long-winded hexameters.

Queen of the Sunrise, he intoned, *Mistress of the Evening Star,*

Pearl of the Sunset, O much beloved Lady, outshining even
The resplendent eyes of the cow-eyed Juno...

He continued in this vein until I lifted a hand to stop him; his fulsome apostrophe came to a squawking finish. "I can see you are a poet," I said.

"Yes," he said, "I've written a poem even longer than the *Aeneid.*"

"By the Muses," I said, "what subject could merit such treatment?"

"The Punic Wars, Divinitas," he said.

"Well, I suppose it is safe to impugn the Carthaginians," I said, "since they can't impugn us back."

I am not sure he realized I was making fun of him, but he changed the subject. "Otho," he said, "the Senate commands you to join the consular embassy to Galba."

"I'll have to go," Otho said. "If I don't kiss his feet, I'll probably find myself kissing the Tarpeian Rock."

"True enough," said Silius Italicus. "A lot of traitors have been flung from that selfsame rock in the last few days." To me he added, "You may remain in Rome, of course, under senatorial protection." Which probably meant a dagger in the night, or, if they were feeling generous, a vial of poison.

"I think I'd feel a little safer with these Praetorians," I said. "I will go with Otho."

***

Otho did not even have a home in Rome, and I did not really want to return to Nero's Golden House, and so we ended up at my villa, well, one of my villas, the one that was once Petronius Arbiter's.

To step into the house where I had last lived as a slave was a strange thing. To be welcomed by Croesus, who had once had the unwilling task of whipping me, filled me with a bitter joy.

The women of the house made much of me, claiming I was too thin and bringing me a stuffed mouse from the kitchen, dripping with honey and garum. Hylas was smiling to see old friends. Shortly afterwards, Marcus Vinicius arrived and embraced me warmly. This was the only place in the world that felt like a home to me.

"Shall I put Marcus Salvius Otho in the cubiculum of the former dominus?" Croesus said.

Before Otho could reply, I said, "I would prefer Petronius's chamber always to remain as it was."

"Another room, then," said Croesus. "We do have several more, you know."

The evening meal was a little strained. I sat as host, alongside Marcus and Croesus, whose status was of course no longer that of a servant. And I was at the center of the head triclinium, my status not dependent on any master, lover, or husband. And Otho was being entertained as my own guest, not as a visiting dignitary. I was not there to sit on his lap and smile flirtatiously. We had fresh delicati to do that job, for Croesus had filled all the household positions vacated by Petronius's death, manumissions, and my departure to the royal palace.

Petronius had always had two delicati in his service; when I came I had been the supernumerary. Croesus had found examples more exotic even than I had been, beautiful creatures from beyond the edge of the Empire. One was dark as night, and the other pale as snow with almond eyes. Otho was not displeased. For Marcus Vinicius, there were also girls, one skinny and one voluptuous. And if Croesus could sit at my table, then so could Hylas. He did, awkwardly.

No one talked. A girl of the Aksumites, who come from Ethiopia, played on a tortoiseshell lyre and sang in an unknown tongue, accompanied by boys playing finger cymbals and a little drum. The song was lyrical, full of twisted melismas.

During dinner, which was a simple affair with only around a dozen courses, we had local wine, Falernian, well diluted with water; afterwards, a Greek wine, Chian I think, drunk inappropriately neat, for we needed something to break the tension.

It was Otho who snapped first. He flung his kylix across the room and it smashed on the mosaic stones. He began weeping uncontrollably. "He was my friend," he kept repeating.

Croesus said softly, "He stole your wife, and exiled you to Lusitania."

"My wife's right here," he said, gripping me by the shoulders.

"Your wife," Croesus said.

Otho looked at me.

"I was with Poppaea when it happened," I said.

"He was my friend," Otho said.

But the Gods do not have friends, I thought.

"We leave at dawn," I said. "If you don't align yourself with Galba before he reaches Rome, you are done for."

***

I lay in Petronius's chamber. But I could not sleep. I could hear poetry from his lips take wing: his own, but also the ancient lyric poets, Sappho, Alcaeus, and the modern ones like Ovid; those words, weighted by memory, hung in the air. I yearned to be hugged by my old master, to fall asleep to the rhythm of his breathing.

Around the sixth hour of the night, I realized I could never sleep with all those ghosts. I sprang up; Hylas, on the floor next to me, rubbed his eyes, threw a sheer cloth over my shoulders, and lit a lamp, and followed me out into the hall, so quietly I knew he was there only by the flickering light he held out.

I stumbled at random through the portico, into the atrium, among the trees and the herms, pallid in the soft moonlight. And in this way, I found myself in a guest chamber, where Otho lay, not sleeping either.

"My beloved," he murmured.

What a vision he must have seen. Me, a silhouette against the lamplight, the fabric already slipping down my chest and pooling on the tiles.

Me, impossibly beautiful, more dream than flesh.

"You don't know how I longed for you, Poppaea," he said. "In Lusitania the Celtiberian boys are renowned for their lubricity, but they were not you."

"I am not Poppaea either," I said.

"No, not the Poppaea of the stinking flesh," he said. "You're the Platonic perfection of Poppaea, the face of a goddess and the loins of a god. Oh, but you broke into my dreams, you troubled my waking thoughts."

I walked toward him. I no longer had the wherewithal to return his desire. But I felt pity. And so I let him take me into his arms. He was not pleasing to me. He had a stale smell, and it did not blend well with all that Chian wine. Understanding my distaste, Hylas blew out the lamp so I would not have to look at him. I try not to remember what followed. I sent my mind to a place far, far away.

***

But this was not your first time with him.

It was and it was not. For when I joined him and Poppaea in their unhappy bed, I was a slave. I existed to be used, as a tool to salve Otho's inadequacies and Poppaea's needs. I needed to please him, because my master sent me and I always yearned for Petronius's approval.

That night, I was permitted to feel disgust, to feel ill-used, because I was free, a human being. The mechanics were the same, but I had free will. Yet I still let him do whatever he wanted. He lurched, he flailed, he cried out. And I made myself feel nothing. And when his ecstasy was spent and he fell into a deep sleep, Hylas led me to my private caldarium, and I tried to soak away every trace of him from my body.

You didn't love Otho even a little?

It is strange. I loved Petronius. That is obvious. But I also loved Poppaea for her wit and deviousness, and because, while helping her own cause, she felt for me a little. I loved my fellow slaves whom I later owned. And there was Nero. He was a monster, and yet, there were little ways in which he made you love him despite his madness. There were moments of purity, of clarity. Only in his death did I truly understand the words of Catullus: *Odi et amo* ... how love and hate could be so inextricably intertwined.

But Otho? I did not love Otho.

That night I realized that I was never going to love anyone again.

It was going to be about survival from now on. Only survival mattered.

XXVII

Galba

We'd wasted some time delivering the dead Divinitas to the Senate, and spending the night in my villa. It only took a week to reach Galba's encampment, as he had already crossed the Po. For speed, and because we weren't going to fight anyone, we only took only one maniple of cavalry, and I finally got used to a horse. I think Otho picked the gentlest one he could for me. Always considerate of my pace, Otho did not force the cavalry more than thirty miles a day.

The stench came first, when the walls of the castra were not even in sight. And we could see scavenger birds in the distance.

Otho said, "He's been busy crucifying people. You can smell it from here."

As we got closer we could hear the pounding of nails and the grunt of legionaries hoisting crosses. Otho had sent a messenger ahead, and our man returned with a legate from the castra, to make appropriate greeting and to lead us in. And presently, at the wooden gate, Galba was there himself, the very picture of a military man.

The reek had become overwhelming and now we saw a forest of crosses; they were recent, for most of the men, women and children who had been strung up were still alive, and some were not too weak to still be groaning.

"Hail, Caesar," Otho said, acknowledging reality for the present.

"I'm terribly sorry about the mess," said the General. "But you know how things work. Setting an example."

"Crucifying children?" I gasped.

"If slaughtering one village can buy the allegiance of a thousand …" said Galba. "Besides, they weren't citizens."

"You should show some respect to the Dowager Empress," Otho said.

"You're pathetic," Galba said. He turned to his legate. "Take the boy and find him some proper clothes."

I got off my horse — or rather, was helped off — but as I was being led away, I overheard more of the conversation.

"There's going to be no more chaos, Otho," Galba was saying. "People will confine themselves to their proper station in society. Cross-dressing will be confined to the home, or to designated brothels. Only the anuses of slaves and social inferiors will be violated. Women will no longer meddle in politics." He continued in that vein until I was out of earshot.

Galba was not going to be a popular Emperor, that was certain.

***

Our entry into Rome was the reverse of my previous triumph. The crowd outside the city was sullen. Many looked away. Galba rode ahead. Otho rode just behind.

I was in the entourage that followed him, but not in a position of prominence. I wore a simple tunic, my hair no longer coifed, my face no longer whited with lead paint. No one recognized me without my royal regalia. I was just some superannuated delicatus, without any skills, and no longer capable of growing up into a whole man.

As we entered, however, the crowd grew, though they still said nothing. Presently someone cried out, "Isn't that Otho, Nero's friend?"

Galba turned. A centurion stepped out of the ranks and slapped the man's face.

Otho rode up to Galba and whispered something. Galba motioned. Two soldiers rode forward, each carrying a hefty sack. They began tossing silver denarii into the mob. And finally the cheering started.

I heard someone say, "This one's real, not the debased crap the last Emperor was shitting out!"

"Ave Caesar! Please lift the piss tax!"

"Ave Caesar! Double the bread dole!"

At last, in the distance, we could hear shouts of "Galba! Galba! Galba!" Perhaps someone from the Senate had come out to coach the mob.

When the soldiers ran out of coins, more were brought up from the back. As we approached the Forum, people were filing into the square now. It was still not what you might call crowded, but the denarii were having a real effect. Gold would have been better, but these were not prosperous times.

What can I say? We reached the Curia Julia, and this time the Senate were out in force, standing before the huge bronze portals which had been flung wide open, revealing the Augustus's pristine white marble within.

The crowd were yelling full-throatedly by now, as much in fear as in enthusiasm. This time I watched a living Emperor enter the Senate, not a dead one.

I wished never to see him again. It was one of the few wishes I ever had in life that was actually granted.

And so it was that I returned to my own villa, as I had come to think of it.

But I could not live out my days in quiet luxury. For one thing, I had acquired a house guest. Marcus Salvius Otho, husband of the woman I looked like, former friend of a disgraced Emperor, former governor of Lusitania, followed me back to the house. He had no home in Rome, and I did not have the heart to send him away.

Except from my bed; that night I asked my slaves to watch the door to my cubiculum, and slept with Hylas in my arms, clutching him to my bosom, like a child with a favorite toy.

***

I had known from the moment I heard him muttering about restoring morality, that day in his castra, that Galba would not be well-liked. For one thing, he made no effort to revoke the damnatio memoriae which had been pronounced on the late Divinitas, and had allowed only a skimpy state funeral, without even any games.

Not only was the urine tax not repealed, but there was an even worse problem.

It was Marcus Vinicius who told us about it, and it was a problem we should all have foreseen.

It was at another of those nerve-wracking dinners, with Otho gazing longingly at me while the entertainment danced and sang. With no special guests, the repast was really simple; I had forbidden the slaves to serve more than five courses and to hold the dormice for higher-profile visitors.

"Why can't *I* have a dormouse?" Otho was complaining. "It's not as if you can't afford it, Poppaea."

"Don't call me Poppaea anymore. I am Gaius Petronius Gaii Libertus Sporus again now, Marcus Salvius Otho," I said. "The Divinitas said no more gender-hopping. I was there, I heard it."

Otho seemed oblivious. "We need to get married," he said.

"Why?" I said. "You're not planning to seize the principate. You don't need *me* for any kind of twisted justification. You don't need to live in Rome. Don't you have estates?"

"Nero made sure I was starved for resources and stuck in Lusitania. It was all I could do to pay these few Praetorians who came with me to dispose of Nymphidius. Poppaea owned everything and ... in effect, *you* are Poppaea now, by the fiat of the Divine Nero."

"And marrying Poppaea would get you all your property back ... and give you a shot at the throne, however far-fetched," I said.

"I love you," he said, tearing off a hefty hunk of bread and swallowing it with some wine and olives. And we did not speak for a long while, but ate in silence.

It was at that point that Marcus Vinicius arrived and was ushered into the triclinium. He kissed me on the cheek and sat down on my left, and without any further salutation, said, "Galba is doomed."

"But," Otho said, "he's only been Emperor for two months."

"It's the donativum," said Marcus. "The army hasn't been paid."

"Why not?" Otho said. "When a new Emperor is proclaimed, there is always a donativum to the army. Nero's was excessive, at 3,750 denarii, and bankrupted the treasury for years. He was forced to debase the currency."

"Nymphidius promised them double that, and Galba won't pay it."

"Seventy-five hundred denarii?" Otho said.

"Each," said Marcus Vinicius.

The normal salary of an ordinary soldier is two hundred and twenty-five denarii per year. This offer, therefore, was like paying every soldier thirty-five years' wages.

"What could he have been thinking?" Otho said. "I would not dare promise that much, if they made *me* Emperor."

"How much?" said Marcus Vinicius.

"Well ... just hypothetically ... I might pay twelve hundred and fifty ... and that would be extreme, for the Divine Augustus gave a donativum of only two hundred and fifty and that was not upon his accession — it was in his will."

"I will convey your offer to the Praetorians," Marcus said, rising from the table.

"Wait!" Otho said. "I haven't *offered* anything to anyone."

But Marcus Vinicius was already on his way out, and Hylas was handing him his sword and helmet.

I said to Otho, "That was foolish."

"It would be nice to get my estates back," he said softly. "And to be able to appear in public with my wife."

"I'm not your wife."

"I want you," he said.

I despaired of ever being allowed to be my true self. I took a gulp of undiluted wine, so quickly I could barely keep it down. "I suppose you'll have to become Emperor then," I sighed.

Damnatio Memoriae · 198

XXVIII

Domus Aurea

For most people, the assassination of an Emperor is unthinkable. For me, it had become almost commonplace.

I had seen — some would say, participated in — the killing of my late husband.

I had been relieved, if not actually taken pleasure, at the murder of Nymphidius in the moment when he was about to mount me.

I did not really relish being present at the death of a third. Especially since both previous deaths had occurred while the princeps, or would-be princeps, was attempting to make love to me.

Fortunately, I was probably not to Galba's taste, and so Otho did not need me to lure the current Caesar to some sordid tryst. The murder of Galba was accomplished by one thing only: money.

And not even real money; just Galba's refusal to pay what Nymphidius had promised, and Otho's lesser proffer being deemed more reliable, and better than nothing.

So it was that less than three months after his triumphant entry into the Senate, the spineless and ineffectual Otho succeeded in engineering the Emperor's demise.

He did not give me any details.

He merely pushed past the guards at my door and interrupted my breakfast. "It's done," he said. "Have your slaves pick out something pretty for you to wear."

"Where are we going?" I said.

"Home," said Otho.

"Home?"

"To the Golden House."

Once again ... *my* home. Not Otho's.

***

Later I would be told how Galba had been lured to the Forum, and how not a single Praetorian defended him — though a few hapless Germans did, not understanding our politics. A minor battle had raged in the Forum.

I heard about his head being displayed on a spike to mocking boys who had ridiculed his virility, then later sold to his daughter. But I had only seen and heard Galba that once, so it meant nothing to me.

Otho had been proclaimed Emperor by the Praetorians, carried on their shoulders into the Curia, and the Senate had little choice but to vote to grant him full Imperium. Otho did the right thing, having a hundred and twenty people executed for killing Galba, thus deflecting responsibility for the assassination from himself.

The flaw in all this was that Otho had had to promise to make good on Nymphidius's donativum....

***

And so I returned to the Golden House of Nero.

The house of three hundred rooms. The house with the secret garden at its summit.

Those who greeted us were familiar to me. Epaphroditus, who could not be disposed of because he alone knew where every document was. Epictetus, still limping, still philosophizing. Old Spider, now living in the bowels of the palace. These were people who cared for me. There was even Hercules the cheetah, who had gone a little mad in my absence, but started to calm down as soon as he detected my familiar scent.

So this vast palace, robbed of its flawed soul since the death of Nero, was also home to me. Having nothing, I now possessed more than I ever had when I was the plaything of a god.

I came dressed in the best finery that could be found in Petronius's house. Here, there was nothing for me but to live the image of a Goddess.

Otho was a diligent Emperor. To everyone's surprise, he was an even-handed ruler. The mob had known him as Nero's friend, and they even started to call him Nero Otho. I was accepted as Empress, with the occasional snigger mind you, but no one really objected. My possession of a penis was a minor foible. My presence gave a veneer of continuity to Otho's rule. The games came back and the bread dole was doubled. Things were, if not actually utopian, at the very least calm.

You would think that Otho would continue to rule for decades; things were more stable than they had been under any of the later Julio-Claudians. But of course, there was one thing that hung over his head, one Damoclean flaw ... Otho had not yet paid the army donativum promised by Nymphidius. Not the seventy-five hundred denarii, not even the twelve hundred and fifty he had agreed to. The treasury would not have borne it without tripling the taxes.

Each morning, Otho went to work, taking petitions and supplications, religiously attending the Senate, officiating at state sacrifices, opening games. I usually dined alone, and saw Otho only in the dead of night.

Each night, I suffered his attentions, doing my best to please him or at least not to offend; each morning I was thankful to have survived another day.

And in the daytime, I wandered through the palace. Sometimes with Hylas, sometimes only with the cheetah. The Divine Nero had built this place with infinite imagination and cunning, and it seemed I was the only one there to appreciate it.

There were hidden grottoes underground, illumined by eerie blue light; there were libraries with diligent curators and no visitors; there was a theater designed for an exclusive audience of one guest with attendants; there was even a private lupanar with a fine selection of perfect women and boys, and not a single customer. I spoke to Epaphroditus about it, and he quietly sold off the whores; I used the money to redecorate the area as another private dining room.

And everywhere, there were images of Nero. He was painted on walls. There were statues. There was a mosaic with Nero as Apollo, strumming on a kithara.

The Golden House stretched from the Palatine to the Esquiline. There were underground passageways, stairways to unexpected vistas. There were fountains. There were treasure chambers. There were cubicula that had never been slept in, and slave quarters whence the slaves had never been summoned to perform any tasks.

Everywhere, even in hidden corridors, I saw images of my former husband.

There were never any images of Otho. Otho was Emperor, but in this palace he was invisible.

Growing bolder, knowing no one could stop me, I started to wander the city with a small escort, sharing a litter with Hylas. Everywhere we went, the crowds steered clear, for soldiers went in advance to move the populace out of the way. Near the Circus there was a towering statue without a head.

Elsewhere, images of Nero had been defaced, scrawled over with graffiti.

"I know you are thinking of him," Hylas said. "I know where they keep him." And he directed the litter-bearers to take us to the Pincian Hill, in the northeast corner of the city. I was not familiar with these streets and wondered how Hylas had come to know of them.

We found ourselves at the entrance to a mausoleum. A veiled woman stood guard. It took a moment to recognize her as Actë, for this building was the resting place of the Domitii Ahenobarbi, Nero's family before he was adopted into the Julio-Claudians; few remembered his birth name was Lucius Domitius Ahenobarbus.

"This is what I do now," she said. "I watch over Lucius's tomb."

Actë was not only veiled, but wore the plain white robes of a priestess. This place was a hidden temple to a man whom the Senate had not deified. No one had dared to invade this private mausoleum.

I hadn't even known Himself had been decently buried. I had imagined the vengeful Senate throwing his body to the beasts, or leaving it to rot somewhere.

This peaceful place was not what I had thought to find.

"Let me take you to see him," Actë said. She took me by the hand and led me through a low gate to a garden. A statue of Himself, not decapitated, stood at its center. A small temple lay beyond. Actë went on ahead and I followed.

There was a circular chamber within. Another statue of Nero stood watch, with incense and an altar.

The tomb itself was simple; it had probably been someone else's tomb, hastily re-carved. Another woman tended an altar-flame. I was again surprised to see who it was: Statilia Messalina, Nero's only surviving properly married wife of the appropriate gender.

I had barely seen her; she had never lived with us, and had existed purely as a convenience. Now she, too, was here, veiled and robed as a priestess.

"You could join us if you wanted to, Sporus," she said. "History has cast us aside; here we can be at peace."

I wasn't quite ready to retire from life itself.

As you know, I am not even twenty years old yet, and I then, no reason to believe I could not continue to survive somehow.

I put my hand on the sarcophagus. A frieze had been sculpted around it, not with any great skill, for the artist had worked in haste. It depicted the major incidents of Nero's life. His elevation at the hands of Claudius. His much-vaunted war in Britannia and the quashing of Boudicca's rebellion, which he had not even been present at. His building of amphitheaters. His victory in the Olympics. His mother. His wives ... Poppaea and Statilia. Actë was not depicted, and neither was I. We were not part of the official history.

I stroked Poppaea's marble face.

"How can he have a temple, when he isn't a god?" I asked no one in particular.

Actë said, "The Senate doesn't *really* create the gods, you know. We do, in our own hearts."

I sacrificed a dove to Himself; they were kept in cages in a back room.

We heard a fanfare from outside. Someone important was arriving with the full panoply of state.

Announced by a quartet of cornua, preceded by a dozen Praetorians, it was Otho who entered.

"There you are, my dear," he said. Not to me, but to Statilia Messalina. "The Senate has urged that I take a female wife to clarify the line of succession, and I can think of no one better than you."

"You'll divorce me?" I said, not without a glimmer of hope.

"Of course not. You're still my one true love. But the Senate thinks that in public at least — at state functions — a wife without a penis might be more viable politically."

"I might have one of those," I said, "but the Divine Nero made sure I would never grow into a man."

"Statilia, you will keep the throne warm for me while I am gone," Otho said. "While my beloved Poppaea-with-a-penis will warm me on campaign."

"Campaign?" I said.

It was then that I learned that we had used up all the good will from the army that came from my association with Himself the late Divinitas. The ill will from not paying the donativum had continued to fester, and now, as it were, the boil had burst.

"I should have paid the seventy-five hundred," said Otho.

The army in Germania had declared their own general, Vitellius, Emperor, and it was up to Otho to lead his as-yet unpaid and very displeased troops north to do battle. The civil war of succession, paused when General Galba had defeated Vindex and when Otho had slain Nymphidius, was now back in full swing.

Damnatio Memoriae · 208

XXIX

Civil War

Thus it was that in my short life's winter I finally saw war, the thing that drives the human experience.

I had heard a thousand songs about the glory. *Dulce et decorum est pro patria mori,* Horatius Flaccus rhapsodized. Julius Caesar said *Veni, vidi, vici,* and Romans frequently repeat that *audaces fortuna juvat.* Fortune favors the bold.

The Greeks, four centuries ago, knew better, it seems. Euripides called war *ta megista kaka ton anthropon* ... the greatest evils of the human race. He defined it as "a man, and the beginning of death." Petronius had filled my brain with so much poetry, yet I had never imagined the blood.

The screaming. The hacked-off limbs. Boots tramping through bloody mud. The clash and the clang of it.

Before that, there was a short voyage; we set sail up the coast in order to shorten the distance to cut off Vitellius before he could march all the way down to Rome. Otho journeyed in style, with every luxury brought with us from the Golden House: soft couches, an Imperial cook, livestock for fine dining, and a supply of body-slaves and masseuses; the Imperial secretaries, headed by Epaphroditus, were with us as well. As for me, I only had Hylas, but at the last moment had brought Hercules as well, as the cheetah had been lonely in my absence, and had acquired a vicious streak, devouring one of the maids' children. With me, he was always sedate, and of course, well fed.

We were joined by legions from Dalmatia, Pannonia and Moesia, and we had the Praetorians; there seemed to be little reason not to prevail against legions who had been made to force-march from the Rhine, and were probably eked out with mercenaries from Germania.

But the omens were not very auspicious.

A white ox slaughtered upon landfall had two livers. An eagle fell dead out of the sky at Otho's feet as we rode inland.

I had briefly been in Galba's castra, but that was just a miniature one, an advance party from his army. Since I was being dragged about by soldiers, I didn't see much anyway.

My first experience of a full-blown Roman camp was that it was much like Rome itself — filled with food vendors and blacksmiths and other tradesmen; but it was all much more orderly, less chaotic, than the city; the avenues were wide and straight; the soldiers knew what they were doing, and had conjured the castra into being in just an hour or two.

There weren't many women. Soldiers were not allowed to marry until they retired. Some kept a woman, or shared one with friends. But the camp boys were a more common sight. Many soldiers kept one, brought from home or picked up as booty from some village. They were just as warm in the night, and could be left to run wild in the day.

It was boys like these that had mocked and jeered at Galba's decapitated head.

If there was one thing that was different about this city of tents, it was that it reeked of masculinity.

"Don't be too curious," Otho told me. "And stay in the tent when we go into battle. You'll have people to keep you safe."

At the first battle, we could not hold the invaders at the Po, and they thrust right past Otho's army, deeper into Italy.

I did not witness the battle, of course. But I did not want to be cooped up in the Imperial tent for the duration of the civil war. And so, restless, I went to see the aftermath.

But I had my first experience of walking at dawn through a field of the dead. I had left Otho's tent in haste, without the elaborate transformation into a Queen. Instead, I dressed as a member of the military. Doubtless I was the envy of the urchins who thronged the camp.

I had my bearers carry me to the field, then walked on on foot.

It had been more of a skirmish than I battle, I was told later, but it was overwhelming. The dead were strewn about in heaps. Loose arms and legs were scattered among them. Flies buzzed and there were birds everywhere, pecking at eyes and wounds. And dogs.

Against the rising sun, I saw a kneeling man, eyes raised toward Heaven, a man in his fifties, perhaps, in a white robe.

"Doesn't he remind you of Simon?" Hylas said, and ran over there, heedless of his caligae squishing dead human flesh.

Curiously, I followed my freedman. I saw nothing to remind me of the boy I had last seen being eaten by lions in the Circus. Unless it was the way the man prayed, swaying and muttering.

"Are you a Jew?" I asked him.

"Not exactly," he said.

I knew then what Hylas had seen; this man was one of the Chrestianoi. I wondered how he had managed to avoid being sent to the arena. Perhaps he had mouthed the obligatory formula of worship to Rome's god's at the last minute.

"Is it safe," I said, "for people like you to be here?"

"Safe? The army is full of us. With the Mithras people and the Sol Invictus followers and the worshippers of rocks and stones, nobody notices another Eastern cult."

I supposed that, with death around every corner, any religion that promised instant salvation would be desirable.

The man, whose name was Josephus, told me that he was a repairer of hipposandals and saddles, and he was in business for himself.

"Why are you praying in the midst of corpses?" I said.

"I don't know. I think I was waiting for you," he said.

"You don't even know me," I said.

"But my dominus does."

"You're a slave, then." Many masters allowed their slaves to run their own businesses and received a share of the profits.

Josephus said, "We are all slaves. Even you. Especially you, because the events that shape you cannot be controlled by you. You will die soon, you know. But before you do so, you should taste Divine Love."

I laughed bitterly. "I have," I said, "and from more than one Divinitas."

"Listen," he said. "I may have lost my looks, but I too was once a delicatus. My master was a centurion in Judaea. You've heard of the place."

I remembered Pontius Pilate going on and on about what a troublesome province it had been. And how he had crucified the leader of these Chrestianoi. "I have," I said.

"My master bought me from a family who had been made destitute by all those those Hasmonean taxes. I didn't want to be sold, but he treated me well; he truly cherished me. My family taught me that most of the world's sexual practices are abominations, but my master never let me feel like an object. I loved him as much as a slave can love a master; he loved me more than that, I think. But I became deathly ill. My dominus told me there was a healer who could cure any sickness, but I told him I was on my deathbed. Still, he insisted on seeking out this so-called prophet, so I kissed him goodbye, and waited to die. Some days passed, I think. I drifted in and out of consciousness. And then something happened...."

"What? Some charlatan waved a wand over you? A witch gave you a magic herb?"

"No ... I was lying there in my misery. And then — all of a sudden — it came over me ... a wave of pure love. This love wasn't just warm and tender; like fire, it burned; I felt as though I were being sucked into a raging flame. I knew that this love was death. But then, suddenly, the fever left me. I stood up. There wasn't a trace of the illness. And my dominus had not even come back from seeking out this healer."

"The magician cured you from miles away."

"My dominus told me about it. He said that this prophet wasn't like a Roman priest, with ritual formulae and sacrifices. All he said was, *You came all this way, and you didn't even bring your puer with you.* My master told him that he was confident in the healer's abilities. And the rabbi said, *Go home, then. I've already cured him.*"

"And you lived happily ever after."

"No, no, listen to me. This feeling of absolute love ... it was something real, something so powerful it can transform anything. My own parents, who sold me to feed themselves, called me a whore, an abomination. Where I come from, no decent person would bestir themselves to help a puer delicatus. It wasn't my fault, but still, I had betrayed my faith and my culture and gone over to the Romans. Even before the Romans came, our land was only a reluctant participant in the Hellenistic world. That's why we're seen as backward, barbaric, clinging to an unfashionable religion.

"In that moment, you see, I became truly myself. And I've tried to let others achieve that transformation, too. The Romans crucified him, you know. But I learned that every love we feel is an echo of Divine Love. The world will end soon, you know. The Beast has already been slain."

"The Beast?"

"Your late husband."

"I was there when he died," I said. "This wasn't a noble sacrifice to bring about a new age. It was something sordid."

"The highest Heaven's foundations rest in the depths of Hell," he said. "You can't touch the stars unless your feet are firmly planted on the earth."

I took Hylas's hand and we left the man praying for his delusions.

***

During the night I was plagued with bad dreams.

More vividly than ever before, I saw my childhood. My mother. The homely sounds of my native language, a language for which the Romans did not even have a name.

I saw the fire and the pirates. I relived the violation on the ship. And once again in my dream I entered the half-world of the dead and came face to face with Pluto, the death-god, greeting me as his bride.

Pluto who was Nero, demanding that I lobby the Senate to admit him to Olympus. "If no one worships me," he said, "how shall I survive in the underworld?"

And in the dream I'm telling him: "I visited your tomb. There was a temple. I sacrificed a dove to you. Actë and Statilia are your priestesses."

"Only two to worship, out of the whole world that once lay at my feet?"

"They will *all* worship you, Divinitas. I'd stake my life on it."

"You'd die for me, my sweet little boy-wife?" said the God of the Dead in my dream. And reached for me with ravenous arms, and enveloped me in a thick darkness, snuffing out my breath until —

And in the morning, we struck camp and moved on to the next battle, which would be at a place called Bedriacum.

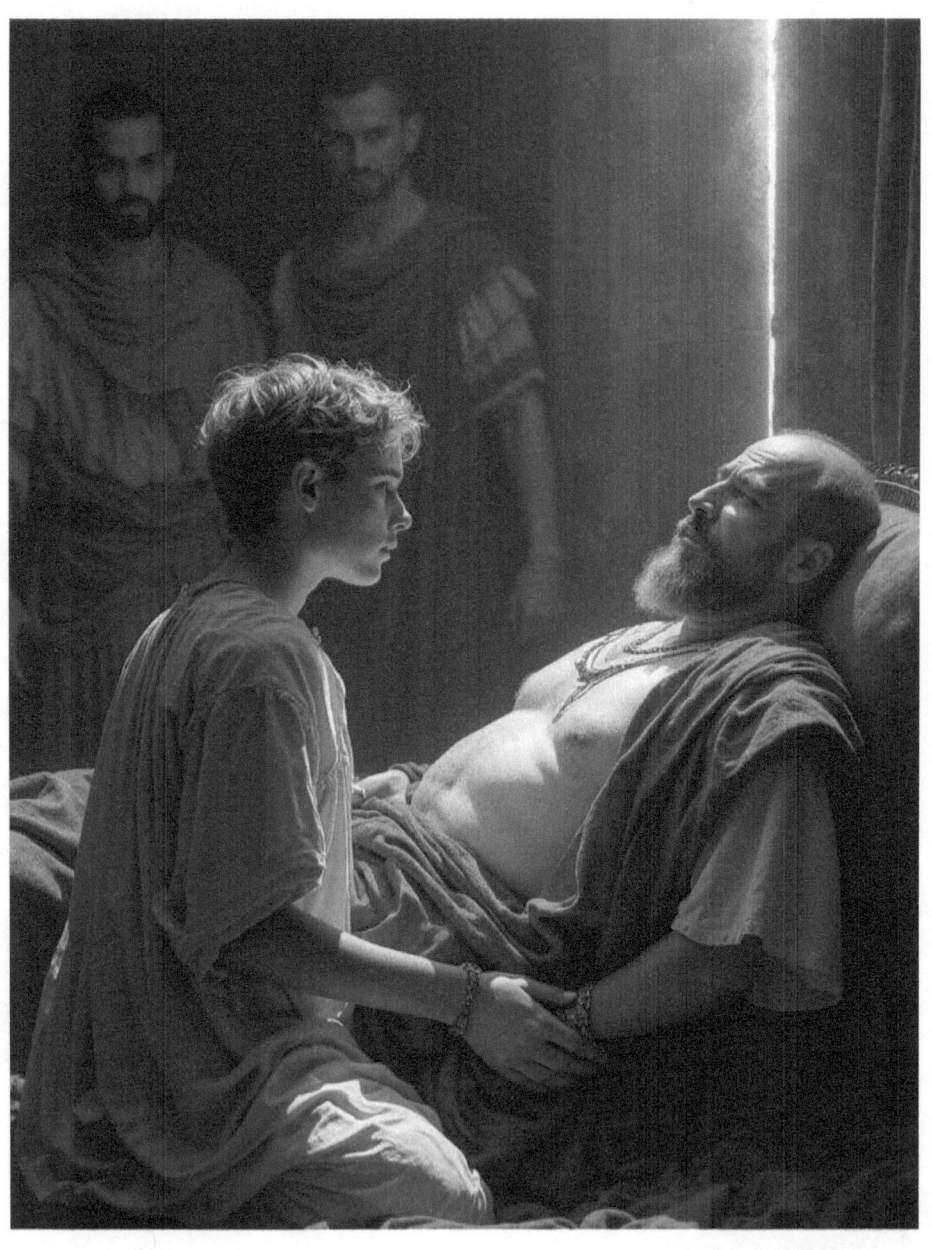

XXX

BEDRIACUM

Yet every battle is the same: more corpses, more harrowing amputations in the field hospital, more wailing, bereaved lovers. By all accounts we were winning, but it weighed heavily on Otho.

I did not go back to the battlefield again. I knew I would find that deluded Chrestianos raving about Divine Love, while scavengers feasted on the dead. I had been curious, but after a few more days of the campaign I did not leave the tent anymore. When Otho came from the field he performed a perfunctory coupling with me, then fell to snoring. I had become something on a list of daily tasks. He took no joy in me, though he murmured *Poppaea, Poppaea,* in his sleep.

Otho had gone through the motions of fighting with one foot already in the grave.

I sat in the tent and made myself beautiful, surrounded by my confidants and Otho's hangers on. One evening I sat quietly while his generals argued. Push ahead! You already have them on the run! No, wait for the Dalmatian legion to arrive, save your men for a bigger battle. And Otho, swayed by both sides, agreeing with first one, then the other.

This would not end well and when Otho decided, quite arbitrarily, on a major battle near the village of Bedriacum. We had moved our camp there. It was a pleasant little village.

The Dalmatian legions had almost arrived ... they were no farther away than Aquileia. But Otho did not want further delay. I watched the army march out of the camp and waited in the tent.

By the afternoon, the camp was filled to overflowing with wounded. It was chaos. Though I had confined myself to the Imperial tent, I could hear the madness closing in on me.

When Otho entered, I could tell he had already given up.

Several of his officers followed him in. "Don't, my Lord," they were saying. "We still have a very good chance of winning."

Otho sat. Hylas poured him wine. There was bread. He dipped a hunk in salt and downed the whole krater of wine.

"Yes, Marcus Salvius," I said. "We might win."

Otho was the only security I could cling to now. I had to prevent him from giving up. But he only said, "Yes, my darling, we *might* win. But we'd still be in a civil war. It will only end if there's only one claimant to the Empire left standing."

"But you've been a good Emperor," I said.

"I haven't paid the army," he said. "I don't know where that money would come from. Someone craftier than I must balance that equation."

"But Marcus —" I said.

"No, no, my dearest Poppaea. The proper Roman thing to do in this circumstance is to commit suicide. I would retain my honor; my property, meagre though it is, could go to my heirs, such as they are. I'll get a decent funeral, and a decent cranny of the afterlife to inhabit. My mind's made up."

I dreaded what I knew he would ask me next, and he did so anyway. He said, "You're the only person I trust, and I don't want it botched. So please, Poppaea dearest, hold the sword while I run on it."

I was sick to my stomach. "I can't do that, you know I can't," I said. "I'm ... you know, delicate."

"Ita," he said. "Delicate es," he added, correcting my grammar to the feminine form of the adjective. "But you can surely hold a sword without flinching. Look at all the bloodshed you've seen!"

Yes. Why was it so hard for me? Since my enslavement, I had seen crucifixions, beheadings, and people eaten by lions. An Emperor had died in my arms, and a would-be Emperor had been killed while raping me. What was one more dead Emperor?

***

All at once — a clamor from outside! We heard shouts and swords clanging against shields! A few shrieks of dying men. And then, abruptly, silence. Except for the distant whimper of someone being raped. It would not be long.

One of the generals placed a sword in my hands, and angled it upwards, directly at Otho's heart. He steadied me, making sure my grip was firm.

I told myself, *There is no love between me and Otho.* It was not as it had been with Nero, where there was both love and hate in equal measure; Nero and I were bound together by his delusion and my willingness to inhabit it.

I don't love you, I thought. I had only ever pitied him.

And so it was that Otho looked into my eyes and said, "Farewell, my beloved," and "We shall see each other in the next world," and slowly bent down to kiss me; the blade entered him as he embraced me, and as his lips touched mine, the sword-point breached his heart.

For the third time, I was holding a bloody, dying Emperor in my arms.

It was then that the cries of "Hail, Vitellius!" could be heard from all around us. Our men had all gone over to the enemy. Loyalty had been bought, and it was fleeting. The shouting came in waves. We were drowning in an ocean of traitors.

"You see ... why ... now," Otho gasped. "I could not have ... remained."

I knew that Otho had at least attempted to govern well. He had done popular things. But only paying the army their donativum would guarantee stability. And that would have caused Rome to starve to death. It was a dilemma with no viable solution.

We heard the tramp of soldiers' caligae. The tent-flap was ripped open. The victor of the battle stood in the entrance.

I had never seen Vitellius before, but I knew exactly who this must be.

Aulus Vitellius was square-jawed and chubby-cheeked. Otho was overweight, but Vitellius was luxuriantly obese. He was jovial as he walked in; he had been cracking jokes outside.

As he came in, Otho died. He rolled onto the floor. Some of his men hastened to make sure he lay in a dignified position.

Vitellius hardly glanced at him. He only looked at me. I sat there, covered in blood, my makeup not completely done, my clothes ripped. I looked nothing like an Imperatrix.

Certainly not to Vitellius, who said simply, "So this is the much-vaunted cinaedus."

I was probably done for, so I decided to brazen it out. "Don't use such a vulgar word, Aulus Vitellius. I am no one's dirty little catamite. I am the recognized wife of Nero Otho, and until the Senate decrees otherwise, I'm still your Empress."

"Is that so?" Vitellius said, and started to laugh. His men all laughed too. And then Otho's own servants, who had stood by loyally in attendance on his honorable death, also started laughing. Sycophants, the lot of them.

"You're a cheeky one," Vitellius continued. "Don't you realize you're entirely at my mercy? I could have you crucified."

"You won't, though. Despite everyone's efforts to denigrate his name, Nero is still more popular than any of you one-day Emperors. Giving me a slave's death would be politically unwise."

"You have the backbone to threaten me, yet the intelligence to talk sense," Vitellius said. "You're no ordinary catamite."

"Would you like to find out?" I asked him, hoping that a twinge of seduction in my voice would lower my chances of execution.

"Impertinent little savage!" Vitellius said. He slapped me resoundingly. It stung, and I should have fallen off my seat, but I gritted my teeth and glared back at him.

He laughed again.

"I'm not going to kill you," he said at last, "not yet at least. You are entertaining, and what you say has some merit. If I am to rule, I'll need the good will of the Nero-loving mob. Meanwhile ... why don't you make yourself useful? You could take care of the arrangements for your husband's funeral, for example."

"At the expense of the state?" I said.

"You pay for it," he said. "I'm going to have to find a way to eke out the donativum."

I looked down at the body of my most recent husband. Marcus Salvius Otho, known as Nero Otho by the mob, had been Emperor for ninety-one days. It was the shortest reign in the history of the Empire. Unless you count Nymphidius's, which could be numbered in minutes, not days.

I was not chained up, not for now. I was accorded a modicum of dignity. The Imperial secretaries and staff were immediately requisitioned so they could start to brief our new Emperor on the current state of affairs. But I was allowed to keep Hylas with me.

I was given an hour to prepare for the journey back to Rome. Otho's body, as well as my person, were to be among the spoils of this civil war.

As we quit the tent, as I was boarding the cart that would take me to whatever was next for me, I noticed that a few people were being crucified; no more than strictly necessary to show that Vitellius meant business. It was almost an afterthought. There was no one of any importance. I did notice that Chrestianos among them, though, the one who had spoken to me about the incomparable splendor of Divine Love.

XXXI

AULUS VITELLIUS GERMANICUS

So ... Vitellius let you live.
For a while.
Then what are you doing here at the Circus, and why am I being tasked to transform you into the Goddess of Death?

I said for a while.

Do you not understand?

There are philosophers who say that time is a circle, not a line. I say that time can be both a line and, at other times, a recursive circle which you cannot escape from.

For a few months, then, I was neither a condemned criminal nor a revered goddess. Rather, I was under a kind of house arrest. The Senate, of course, declared Aulus Vitellius Emperor, adding the title of Germanicus, though he had not conquered any Germans. Rebuffing the past, he did not take the appellation Caesar as well.

Vitellius did not wed me — not having grown up among the Julio-Claudians, the first Emperor *ever* not to have been born into Senatorial rank, he was somewhat straitlaced when it came to the duties and societal place of men and women, and no room in his mind for any other gender.

However, unless the mob turned against the memory of Nero, who had been the most entertaining of the first five Emperors, he could not exactly get rid of me. Certainly he could not do so quietly, because people would ask questions.

Can you hold still for me? You are restless, Goddess.

And how could I not be? This endless making up is taking its toll. It's one of those endless circles. You make me into a goddess, then you wipe it all off and start again.

Tell me about Vitellius-who-wasn't-called-Caesar, then.

There is not much.

***

Yes, Aulus Vitellius Germanicus was Emperor, and he filled the Praetorians with his own loyalists, but half the army had not declared along with the Senate — these others favored Vespasian, who was still far away, massacring Judaeans in that remote and troublesome province. Vespasian's shadow loomed over Vitellius's Empire. When would Vespasian arrive? When would he seize power? When would the Senate switch sides and grant *him* imperium over the civilized world?

I admit that I too longed for the coming of Vespasian.

Vespasian knew me. He had even flirted with me. He bore me no malice, and I was sure it would be better to be a distant hanger-on in his world than the center of this one.

An astrologer predicted that Vitellius's reign would end. Vitellius had all the astrologers in Rome rounded up and crucified. The madness of absolute power had started to infect him after only a few months.

When people started to gossip that Vespasian was on the march, the tide turned for me as well. Vitellius summoned me to dinner in the Golden House.

When I arrived, I was immediately separated from my entourage, and armed guards came to fetch me. I did not recognize any of their faces. Dinner was in one of the atria, but around us, the Domus Aurea was being dismantled. From a cage, Hercules watched us, looking weak and unfed.

"Frivolous waste," Vitellius said as I was ushered in. "Cheetahs, peacocks ... while the plebeians have to make do with free bread."

"... and Circuses," said one of the other guests.

I saw that it was Pontius Pilatus, whom I had last seen at one of Nero's banquets.

"Indeed, Circuses," Vitellius said. To me, he added, "You remember Pilatus? A washed-up governor? I summoned him in case he could give me some tidbits about the enemy."

"Titus Flavius Vespasianus," said Pilatus. "Glad this 'washed-up governor' can still be of some assistance to the Divine Vitellius."

"I'm well aware that I'm not Divine," Vitellius said. "But I *am* a pragmatist." Then he turned to me. "You know something about Vespasian, don't you?"

"I met him," I said. Had I just been summoned so as to squeeze me for information? That would be a relief. I had lived for several months, never knowing when the axe would fall.

"You more than met him," said Vitellius.

"Perhaps he wanted more," I said. "But I was married."

I became aware that Epaphroditus was standing behind Vitellius, in the shadows. He would not look at me.

"My secretary," Vitellius said, "who knows everything about everyone. What do you have?"

Epaphroditus said, "We have intercepted a letter, written in code, addressed to 'Divina Poppaea.' It says, 'Wait for me, my dear.' What do you have to say about this?"

"I don't know anything about it," I said. "I mean … it was intercepted. How could I know? I am happy never leaving my house, never talking to anyone but when I am summoned."

"Alas, Sporus, the memory of the Divine Nero is no longer an asset to my reign, and neither are you." To Epaphroditus, he said, "I shall tell the Senate that tomorrow, we will act on the long-standing decree of Damnatio Memoriae, and erase the name of Nero from the world."

"Yes, Divinitas," said Epaphroditus, looking at the floor.

"Arrange to raid all the treasuries, money vaults, and assets hidden in temples. Melt the gold from the statues of the gods. We'll find a way to pay the donativum Nymphidius promised."

"It still won't be enough," Epaphroditus said.

"Taxes, then."

"The mob won't like that," I said.

"Oh! The catamite speaks!" said Vitellius. "We'll have to make sure that doesn't happen again."

I should have kept silent.

"What will calm the mob when taxes are too high?" Vitellius said, turning to Pilatus.

"Games, Divinity."

"Then we'd better find a way to kill Nero's memory, raise taxes, *and* entertain the mob all in one action," he said.

So saying, he pulled a ring from his robe and dropped it on the dinner table in front of me.

"Do you recognize this?" he said. "It was found among the late Nero's most prized possessions."

It was the keepsake I had bought Nero in Greece, and it sealed my fate.

I was to become Persephone in the arena.

Damnatio Memoriae · 232

XXXII

Persephone

Yesterday, the editor of the Games invited me into the arena for another rehearsal of my public execution. "It's tomorrow. Very last postponement. *Nothing* can go wrong," he told me. "This has to send a clear message throughout the Empire."

They chained me up, and told me to act "terrified" while my rapist, whom I had already met thanks to you introducing me some days ago, threw himself at me with abandon; he did not perform any actual penetration, as that would be saved for the spectacle itself, though I clearly felt the stiffness of his eagerness for the task.

"Make a big fuss," he whispered in my ear. "I'll try not to hurt you too much. They want a show, and it's got to be to the death, but that wouldn't have been my first choice; I'd rather keep you around for encore performances, if you know what I mean."

"What if I just pass out, and they drag me out?"

"They'll know," he said. "Not much that escapes them. They're experts, and I'm just a slave, doing what I'm told."

An "artistic advisor" — so they called him — was on hand to make sure that the Vestal Virgins would get the best view, and that all his scenery, representing the underworld, was correctly set up.

"Now, listen, Sporus," he said in Greek — he was one of those artists who had not even bothered to learn the barbaric tongue of their conquerors. "You play this with nobility, like a real Queen. Don't scream and wail like a two-obol whore. You're a goddess, and you can tell from our friend's priapic splendor that he's a god. If you display the proper qualities, who knows? The audience might even demand your freedom."

"I *am* free," I said.

"Now *that's* the spirit. Dignity. Nobility. You know who you are. A goddess, daughter of the Earth herself."

After the rehearsal, they took me back to the bowels of the Circus.

***

The first to visit me was Epaphroditus.

He still could not look at me, but he said, "You know I had no choice."

"You have to survive," I said. "All of us do. We use what the Gods have given us. Wealth, power, family. For you, it is wisdom, knowledge, and intellect. But for me ... all I have is my looks."

"You are the thing that men desire," Epaphroditus said. "If Epictetus were here, he would tell you this: you must let go of everything to find some form of peace."

"Beauty is the greatest curse," I said.

"Oh, Sporus," he said, "how you have short-changed yourself! There is so much more to you than physical beauty. Come now, I need your forgiveness."

I forgave him — he desperately needed forgiveness, though for what, he did not tell me — and he left, leaving behind a bag of honey cakes. Perhaps he thought I should die with sweetness on my lips.

***

Then came my real family: Croesus, Marcus Vinicius, Spider, and Hylas. We exchanged few words. I said, "Don't bother to see the show tomorrow; it will never live up to the advance publicity."

They were all weeping. Not me.

Croesus said, "Epaphroditus gave me another letter, one he did not tell Vitellius about. In it, Vespasian says he is looking forward to seeing 'all of Nero's Empresses, especially the little one I flirted with in Greece.'"

Marcus said, "I am going to join him tomorrow. They say he is not far. They say he may meet Vitellius in battle … at Bedriacum."

Bedriacum would always be known as an insignificant village that made and unmade Emperors.

"Be careful," I said.

"Don't worry," Marcus said. "Half the Praetorians are throwing in their lot with Vespasian. They see what he achieved in Judaea, and they see his aristocratic connections."

"Everything that I own, that's still in my name somehow," I said to Croesus, "draw up papers. I want it all to pass to Hylas."

"I don't want anything!" he said. "I want to die with you!"

"Don't be silly," I said. "You have everything to live for." Hylas began to weep inconsolably. I wanted to hug him and tell him everything would be all right. But how could I? My fate was about to be far worse than any of theirs. And yet all I wanted to do was give comfort to another. What was wrong with me? I comforted them all. I hugged each of them many times.

Hylas was the most reluctant to leave. "When I you first met me," he said, "I was just someone else's lips and buttocks. I couldn't even say anything to my owners. You gave me a tongue. You gave me a mind. You gave me freedom."

Then even Hylas left me, and *you* came back, to give me my final, final touches of makeup.

***

And this is how it ends? The premiere satirical poet in the world, the most beautiful woman in the Empire, two Emperors and a would-be Emperor ... and finally now the Bride of Hades?

I hear people have been waiting since dawn to be seated, and my execution is not until late afternoon. There will be gladiatorial bouts, a venation with giraffes and elephants, and a full-scale recreation of the sack of Troy before my deadly defloration.

You have managed to squirm out of so many things.

Perhaps I still will.

Vespasian may arrive in time. It does not seem likely. Even if he should prevail at Bedriacum ... that's not exactly an hour's ride beyond the walls of Rome!

Or, perhaps, my performance could be so breathtaking that the crowd demands I be spared. That does not seem likely either. You see, it isn't just the God who will be violating my soft flesh.

Everyone in Rome has wondered what it was that Petronius felt when I snuggled up to him. How Nero felt when he took his boy-mistress to his bosom. What it was that Otho and Nymphidius felt, that made them attempt to attain an empire just to gain entrance to my body.

And now they will all know. All of Rome, vicariously, will be fucking me today. All of Rome will know what it is like to love a Goddess. How can they make the sign for mercy when they are too busy coming to climax?

No, I am not going to be spared.

What other choices do I have? Shall I bribe you with the title to one of my villas, so you can smuggle me out with the corpses of slain gladiators?

You might consider the honey cakes, Divinitas.

The honey cakes?

... they are poisoned, aren't they?

I may not say.

How much did Epaphroditus pay to get them through?

I may not say.

I daresay he knows where to get the most tasteless, odorless ones, the ones that worked so well on so many of Nero's predecessors. Should I try them? An ignominious end! But at least I would deny Vitellius the satisfaction of a huge propaganda victory against the memory of Nero.

Nero!

I close my eyes and I see him vividly. Nero Claudius Caesar Augustus Germanicus, poetaster and potentate, traitor and tyrant, master of all the world, seated in glory amidst lickspittles and sycophants ... Nero, whom I alone understood.

Oh, you shone brightly in the tawdry grayness of our world! You were magnificent in your corruption, in your self-delusion. You dreamed a new Rome into being, though it was founded on the folly of Narcissus.

If I eat these honey cakes, will I come before your throne?

Or will I enter a world inhabited by such as Petronius, who was the first to treat me not as an object — even though he owned me as an object? Will he touch me tenderly and call me his Giton, his Ganymede?

Or will I be reunited with Hyacinth, to run with him through the hills and forests, speaking the language of an annihilated people, ignorant of the dark and violent Empire beyond the sea?

I have only a few hours to decide how to die. In public or in solitude. In honor or in infamy. By choice or by compulsion. In agony or like gently falling asleep.

Or I could always hope for Vespasian....

Damnatio Memoriae · 240

Afterword from the Author

Just about every historical source — none of which are quite contemporaneous with the events, and all of which have certain agendas — says that Sporus committed suicide.

And yet....

This book was originally a popular serial in the now defunct Amazon *Vella* platform. From the beginning, I've had readers begging me to let Sporus live. Why shouldn't he? He's had a really tough life — a lifetime of tough lives, and he didn't even get out of his teens.

So ... for those friends in particular ... I've left it so maybe, just *maybe,* he got away. One reviewer even asked me not to believe Suetonius, Cassius Dio, and Tacitus, but go with some of the less well-known sources, so as to avoid "breaking his heart" ... and I do hate to break people's hearts!

When you write a novel in the first person, you can't really kill the protagonist off — or how would he be the narrator? I cheated by setting up the circumstances of the narration so that the death could happen after the last page.

But for those of you would like to imagine an escape, a rescue, or an embarrassed cover-up by the editor of the games ... I've left the door very slightly ajar.

Apart from this little (well, *big!*) thing, I've tried to be as historically factual as I could be, while molding the facts to fit the necessary structure of a novel. It's actually mostly the mundane things in this book that are made up out of whole cloth ... getting from incident to incident, coalescing different incidents and of course the initial pirate raid. No one actually know where Sporus came from.

But *really* weird stuff in this novel is often historically attested. The urine tax. The Emperor cheating in the chariot races by using ten horses, not even finishing, yet still winning the first prize.

Even when you remove obvious anti-Nero bias from the incidents described by ancient historians, what remains is still pretty crazy. And yet we are only gradually starting to realize that Nero was in fact a very popular Emperor.

I've tried to treat those things that are outlandish, shocking and immoral to modern sensibilities in the spirit in which the Romans themselves took them. Sex and violence were not the profundities of the human condition that they are in our society today. Rather, they were entertainment.

The universal truths of 1st Century Roman life were quite different. To us, *virtue* is goodness. To the Romans, the noble quality of *virtus* belonged to the penetrator, never the penetratee. Suicide was commonplace and well-respected. Slaves did not object to being raped any more than a chair complained about being sat in. The idea of people being *equal* was perhaps unimaginable.

Yet this was a world in which slaves could, and did, not only become free but arise to positions of immense power. They could be powerful, indeed, even while still being enslaved: there was a whole army of tutors, doctors, accountants, scribes, and other specialized professions where most of the practitioners were in fact owned by someone.

There was a fluidity between being a non-person and a full-fledged human being — and Sporus's life journey, though incredible, was by no means unthinkable.

I became aware of Sporus not through ancient history but in an English class. The legendary Michael Meredith was my teacher and we were discussing Alexander Pope, who satirized a contemporary, gender-fluid member of the aristocracy as "Sporus" — a "painted bug of gold that stinks and stings."

Michael explained to us who Sporus was in ancient history. In Pope's time, the 18th Century, enough people must have heard of Sporus to get the joke. These days, with less classical education going around, I fear not so much.

This character is mostly just a footnote, but for almost six decades I have been wondering: what if *he* were the viewpoint character for the chaos of Nero and its aftermath?

Like many authors, I end up writing books that I would love to read, but no one seems to have written. Thank you for sharing this strange journey with me.

About the Author

Once referred to by the International Herald Tribune as 'the most well-known expatriate Thai in the world,' Somtow Sucharitkul is no longer an expatriate, since he has returned to Thailand after five decades of wandering the world. He is best known as an award-winning novelist and a composer of operas.

Born in Bangkok, Somtow grew up in Europe and was educated at Eton and Cambridge. His first career was in music and in the 1970s, his first return to Asia, he acquired a reputation as a revolutionary composer, the first to combine Thai and Western instruments in radical new sonorities. Conditions in the arts in the region at the time proved so traumatic for the young composer that he suffered a major burnout, emigrated to the United States, and reinvented himself as a novelist.

His earliest novels were in the science fiction field and he soon won the John W. Campbell for Best New Writer as well as being nominated for and winning numerous other awards in the field. But science fiction was not able to contain him and he began to cross into other genres. In his 1984 novel *Vampire Junction*, he injected a new literary inventiveness into the horror genre, in the words of Robert Bloch, author of Psycho, 'skillfully combining the styles of Stephen King, William Burroughs, and the author of the

Revelation to John.' Vampire Junction was voted one of the forty all-time greatest horror books by the Horror Writers' Association, joining established classics like Frankenstein and Dracula. He has also published children's books, a historical novel, and about a hundred works of short fiction.

In the 1990s Somtow became increasingly identified as a uniquely Asian writer with novels such as the semi-autobiographical *Jasmine Nights* and a series of stories noted for a peculiarly Asian brand of magic realism, such as *Dragon's Fin Soup,* which is currently being made into a film directed by Takashi Miike. He recently won the World Fantasy Award, the highest accolade given in the world of fantastic literature, for his novella The *Bird Catcher.* His seventy-plus books have sold about two million copies world-wide. He has been nominated for or won over forty awards in the fields of science fiction, fantasy, and horror.

After becoming a Buddhist monk for a period in 2001, Somtow decided to refocus his attention on the country of his birth, founding Bangkok's first international opera company and returning to music, where he again reinvented himself, this time as a neo-Asian neo-Romantic composer. The Norwegian government commissioned his song cycle *Songs Before Dawn* for the 100th Anniversary of the Nobel Peace Prize, and he composed at the request of the government of Thailand his *Requiem: In Memoriam 9/11* which was dedicated to the victims of the 9/11 tragedy.

According to London's *Opera* magazine, 'in just five years, Somtow has made Bangkok into the operatic hub of

Southeast Asia.' His operas on Thai themes, *Madana* and *Mae Naak*, have been well received by international critics.

Somtow has recently been awarded the 2017 Europa Cultural Achievement Award for his work in bridging eastern and western cultures. In 2020 he returned to science fiction after a twenty-year absence with *Homeworld of the Heart*, a fifth novel in the *Inquestor* series.

In 2023, Somtow was elevated to the status of Thai National Artist by Thailand's Ministry of Culture, and in 2024 he was awarded the status of Public Diplomat by Thailand's Ministry of Foreign Affairs.

S.P. Somtow has published over one hundred books, as well as premiered over a dozen operas which he composed and wrote the libretti for,

To support S.P. Somtow's work, visit his Patreon account at patreon.com/spsomtow.

His website is at www.somtow.com.

www.ingramcontent.com/pod-product-compliance
Lightning Source LLC
Chambersburg PA
CBHW030516080526
44586CB00011B/209